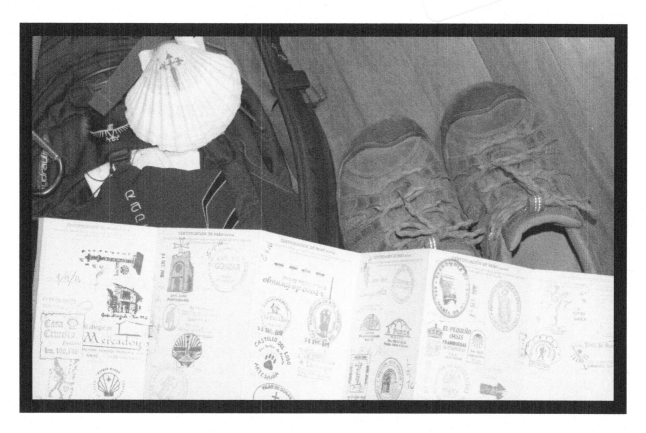

Faithful Metrics

A field guide to measuring ministry without missing the moments

By Peggy Hahn

2017 LEAD

Unless otherwise indicated, all scripture quotations are from the New Revised Standard Version Bible (NRSV), copyright © 1989 by the Division of Christian Education of the National Council of the Churches of Christ in the U.S.A.

Photos were taken by Peggy Hahn during her travels in Spain.

For more information or for bulk orders, contact:
lead@waytolead.org

waytolead.org

ISBN: 978-1981649044

Contents

A Word from the Author

It's the people who love me and whom I love that give my life meaning. For me, sitting at the table with my parents, my children, and my grandchildren provides a window into what makes a meaningful life of faith.

We often wait with hot plates of food in front of us while the older children argue over which grace we will say together. At ages five and six, they have a long list of songs and prayers to choose from. This takes time, while everyone impatiently waits. Once we pray their childhood prayer, my mother chimes in with her prayers. Wow. Everyone sits in silence to listen. For the first time all day, all six children under the age of six are quiet in this moment. Then one of the children interrupts with a loud AMEN and laughter erupts from everyone.

How do we know how to pray as a family?

This is not a rhetorical question. We know because the church taught us to pray. The church keeps us praying even when we have had seasons where mealtime grace was not the norm. We were held through hard, heart-wrenching times when we didn't have words to pray for ourselves and during busy times when we didn't make prayer a priority.

Before long, the children are done eating and leave the table to play nearby. The adults are free to engage in grown-up conversation. My parents reflect on how different things are from when they were parents. They tell stories about their childhood. It makes me remember when my grandmother looked me in the eye and said, "Peggy, this is not my world." She died four years ago at age 93. She was right.

I feel this truth in what my parents are sharing. I can admit that I feel it in myself.

I watch my parents wonder about the dairy-free, gluten-free, vegetarian meals we share together. I share their curiosity about the ways young parents set boundaries on screen time, something we never understood could be helpful when the screen was a television. There are so many new rules; the old rules seem antiquated.

That is until we stop to pray together before meals. Or in those moments when the children ask for (or give) a bedtime blessing.

These practices take my breath away because it is in these sacred moments that I realize what hasn't changed. There is a core way of being that connects the dots between our generations. We are a family that worships, prays, and serves God in the messiness of life.

The power of the Holy Spirit and our home congregations should get all the credit for this. But no one is counting. There is no place for me to tell this story in a way that inspires leaders in the church to keep praying and teaching our traditional prayers (including ones like Johnny Appleseed) to the community.

Instead, the church feels a loss on the weeks we are together as a family practicing our faith outside the walls of our church.

The church feels like it has lost out because we aren't in the room validating the power of the Holy Spirit working in our lives.

I am aching for a church that can find ways to celebrate with us when we have a faith that leaves the building.

I pray for a church that understands, expects, and prepares people to go. Yes ... people go.

Where is the happy dance for people of God sent out to live their faith in daily life? At work, at school, at the table, or at bedtime? This should all count if it is indeed faithful to the Gospel.

Church leaders could stop judging people who miss worship because God is going with them and instead wonder and celebrate all who encounter Christ in these people, all those who will know God's love is for them because people have been sent.

If only we could flip the paradigm with a new value system that encourages going.

The big pushback here is around things no one wants to talk about. Real concerns about funding the salaries of congregational staff, facility maintenance, and programs that teach the faith and serve the poor. These are crucial, right? Or are they? Who decides?

So many of the things I have felt were crucial have turned out to be less than important. If I could reclaim the number of hours I spent ironing my children's church clothes or cleaning and polishing their little shoes so they would look cute at church, it would be shocking how much time I would have had to play and pray with them instead.

We get to lead through a very sacred season in our world where what is kept as a core value and what is released is up for grabs. Some of these decisions are made with God's mission in mind. Others are made to preserve our treasures on earth. There can be a fine line here that is hard to discern.

I love using the lace tablecloth from my deceased mother-in-law or the silver from some relative I never really knew to serve my family dinner. It feels like a perfect blend of values, tradition, and respect made available to my grandchildren, who blow bubbles in the crystal glass filled with milk. In the end, I don't care if they keep the dishes for their own families, but I do care with all of my being that they keep the faith.

Please join me in praying that leaders in the church focus on what matters most. The Holy Spirit is way ahead of us and we are wasting precious time catching .

Peggy Hohn

Uncertainty, Research, and Questions

As leaders in the church today, we are living in the "cone of uncertainty."

For those on the Gulf Coast, this phrase is a red alert that raises anxiety. As the prediction models for the path of the next hurricane become clearer with each passing hour, behavior changes and those in the cone scramble to prepare.

As Christian leaders, we know that the prediction models for the church are all over the place. Forecasts range from "the church is dying" to "the possibilities are endless." Models from the past feel unreliable. Leaders navigating this kind of weather report feel confidence weaken and confusion increase as roles and expectations shift.

How do we know that what we are doing is working? *Is it even faithful to ask this question?*

LEAD has worked with hundreds of congregations over the past few years, learning from leaders who are wrestling out loud with these questions. These are faithful leaders who care deeply and want to do the right thing—but what is it?

On the one hand, leaders know that what they are doing isn't working. Their churches are growing older and smaller every year. Blaming the culture feels like a lie, especially when they listen to the reasons their own children offer for not going to church, things like: "I tried to get involved, but people don't want to try new things." or "There is no one here that cares about what is going on in the world. The church and real life don't intersect."

Leaders are looking at their practices—their very way of "being church"—and asking hard questions. Really hard questions. With heavy hearts. Wanting and not wanting change.

On the other hand, these leaders and congregations are faithful to worship, sacraments, and prayer. They believe in the unmerited grace of God while practicing church inside their cultural comfort zone. Why would or should they have to change or give up something that is so important to them?

This is the tension at the heart of this resource. In LEAD's work with faithful leaders, we recognize a growing conflict between the mainstream culture and a personal preference for church life as we know it. It is out of genuine care for these leaders that LEAD is offering this field guide.

At LEAD, we do not think asking "what does success look like" is unfaithful. We trust that this question comes out of a genuine faith, one that is not throwing theology or liturgy under the bus.

Embracing questions that come from the heart is a way for God's people to discern their call. There is no need to fear the questions. Instead, we can trust that the Holy Spirit is purposefully moving through the cone of uncertainty.

Living through recovery following a natural disaster, churched people can't imagine how unchurched people rebuild their lives. They wonder how others get through the hard times without the confidence that God is in the middle of the crisis. They look at their neighbors and want them to know this God too. It's not that faith is a "happy pill" for post-traumatic stress disorder, but it is a path through the wilderness to a new normal.

Storm survivors know hard decisions must be made along the way that move some things they love into the debris pile in a process called "mucking out." It is a great parallel for congregational leaders who are called to make decisions about what to keep from the past and what to bring into the future. This mucking out process is different for everyone depending on the voices and values that drive the decision-making. If only a single generation, ethnic group, or worldview is heard, their circular feedback creates a downward spiral.

Well-meaning volunteers (or church consultants) who rush in and make quick decisions on behalf of someone else (or a congregation) make matters even worse. The decision-making process essential to discernment of a healthier future is lost.

How can church leaders make good decisions without feedback from a wide audience? Could the current feedback loop be part of the problem?

This field guide is a way forward for faithful leaders who know it is time to make some changes. Mucking out years of ministry debris is every bit as hard as dragging water-soaked sofas, much-loved books, and family photographs to the curb. People do this because they know that mold will set in fast. In no time at all, homes (or congregations) become toxic and once they have become health hazards, nothing can be recovered.

We all have seen congregations that are filled with (figurative) mold. Leaders have waited so long that the only choice is to close. Faithful closing can be celebrated, yet in all honesty, there have likely been moments along the way when leadership missed the opportunity to create a new future.

Through listening, experimenting, and revitalizing congregations, it has become clear to LEAD that faith imagination for church life is held hostage by metrics, members, and mindsets. That tension is paralyzing leaders.

What if leaders are asking the wrong questions? What if the anxieties of a few are keeping leaders from waking up to the Holy Spirit? How do we make the most of these uncertain times?

Although there are Biblical voices that reflect the current despair about the decline in church as we know it, leaders don't find them very comforting.

We all are leading through this in-between time, waiting on God, who seems to be showing up everywhere except in organized religion. Stumbling through the debris is hard, even as we hope to find a few bright spots. There are a number of questions at the core of this uncomfortable season, including the one LEAD is asking in this field guide: How do leaders measure mission without missing the moments?

What are we measuring?

Most of LEAD's work has been in the Evangelical Lutheran Church in America (ELCA). As in most mainline denominations, metrics are perceived to move top down. While they could move bottom up, it seldom happens. The three expressions of the ELCA (congregations, geographic regional groups of congregations called synods, and the national churchwide organization) are a hopeful design that could embrace a relationship with two-way communication across the system. However, when it comes to measurements, those in the local expression of the church rely on the other

levels to ask the questions without ever adding their own. To be blunt, most ELCA congregations let an annual report form drive metrics. LEAD believes that those in the national office would be thrilled if local leaders brought some of their own questions to an annual dashboard or progress report.

This field guide is calling the question: Why don't local leaders set their own metrics? What is stopping this conversation? Leaders have agency to identify questions that can create curiosity about the Holy Spirit's activity in the world, in neighborhoods, in families, and in daily lives. The only thing that limits leaders is a little imagination.

LEAD's research

After wondering about this for over a year, LEAD took another look at the informal research generated by our own work. We have been collecting feedback cards at every speaking gig, every consultation, and every place we visit. In addition, we have been intentionally listening to pastors from the very beginning. Today we are listening with extreme curiosity to pastors in their first call, pastors who are revitalizing congregations, leaders serving communities of poverty, and lay leaders moving into professional leadership. The more we listen, the more curious we become.

One question we always ask is this: What is keeping you from growing as a leader?

The No. 1 answer to this question is:
A lack of confidence.

Without prompting, 60% percent of respondents have written this on a blank line. This drove us to take a closer look.

In January 2017, LEAD worked with the Research and Evaluation Team of the Evangelical Lutheran Church in America to survey a random group of Lutheran pastors. One question offered a list of activities with the invitation to check all that apply: What is the primary area of focus of your ministry?

Potential answers included:
⊕ Helping members learn to tell their personal faith story
⊕ Leading adaptive change
⊕ Teaching spiritual practices
⊕ Creating and empowering teams
⊕ Leading change for the sake of mission
⊕ Leading staff (paid/volunteer)
⊕ Effective communication (external/internal)
⊕ Preaching
⊕ Leading Bible study
⊕ Connecting the congregation to the neighborhood
⊕ Forming disciples
⊕ Casting vision, setting strategic goals for the congregation
⊕ Helping members share the Gospel in their lives

The next question on the survey offered the same list of activities. Respondents were invited to rate each based on this question:

How confident do you feel leading in these areas of ministry?

The result? There was a large gap between the areas of focus that pastors identified as having high value and their confidence as leaders in those areas. The greatest discrepancies were found in these areas:
⊕ Forming disciples
⊕ Effective communication
⊕ Casting vision, setting strategic goals for the congregation
⊕ Helping members share the Gospel in their lives
⊕ Leading change for the sake of mission

This gap between what leaders think is important and what they feel ready to lead is interesting to an organization like LEAD. More important, however, is the overall message church leaders send when they so loudly declare their own lack of confidence. The disruptions in the world and the trends of decline in church membership, worship participation, and giving, have people on edge.

This is understandable. Yet what does the church do when the Holy Spirit is way ahead of its leaders? Most are sick of discussing the problems and are ready for a cure to what ails the church. Yet living in the cone of uncertainty means congregational leaders should be very wary of consultants or any leaders who know exactly what to do and offer technical solutions to adaptive problems.

In this learn-as-you-go world, faithful leadership lies somewhere between a lack of confidence and an arrogant overconfidence. This is a liminal time, a threshold between the past and the future. The Bible is filled with stories of God's people discovering adaptive practices in liminal space.

Are we asking the right questions?

Leading through liminal space requires new questions. Courage for new questions can grow out of the awareness that God is doing a new thing in the new world that is emerging. Shifting mindset is not easy. There are an abundance of possibilities on one hand, and the reality of scarcity on the other. Shifting the mindset of a community of people is even hard. Congregational revitalization requires new questions to spark imagination.

Marilee Adams, in her book *Change Your Questions, Change Your Life: 10 Powerful Tools for Life and Work*, provides powerful tools that can offer a way forward for leaders. She introduces the concept of Question Thinking (QT) to open up possibilities for the shifts that will help leaders move forward.

Adams uses a fable to introduce a very practical, accessible approach to shifting mindset. She uses powerful questions to inspire and motivate positive change, and points out that people have a choice to face issues with either a Judger or a Learner question. A shift from "Why are they saying that?" to "What can I learn from that perspective?" is a simple example. It is surprising to see how a small shift from Judger to Learner questions can open up new possibilities. Adams writes:

> With Judger mindset, the cost can be tremendous. The future can be only a recycled version of the past. And with the Learner program the power is on. The juice is flowing. You can actually make a new future for yourself. (p. 43)

The invitation in this field guide is to move to a Learner mindset as you try changing the questions that impact your metrics. Entering into this liminal space with a curiosity about new questions will help you feel the Holy Spirit moving.

Question Thinking increases your ability to change the future, moment by moment. It provides skills for observing and assessing your present thinking that open up new questions that get better results. *Faithful Metrics* is a plan for congregational Question Thinking.

This is not an answer book but rather a field guide. A field guide is used for journeys without endings. The work of setting faithful metrics will never be completed. As leaders, you can return over and over to the questions of values, goals, purpose, and metrics raised in this resource.

This field guide offers a strategy for you, the reader and leader, to discover your own questions. It is designed for a congregational team, staff, council, or board. The design includes conversation for new learning, opportunities to reflect together, and shared action. This Learn-Reflect-Act model is woven through the field guide in the hope that leaders will intentionally experience this rhythm as a pattern for healthy leaders.

Those reading alone are encouraged to find ways to develop their own personal metrics. Using the rhythm of Learn-Reflect-Act, individuals can become more aware of the people in their lives who influence their personal outcomes. All metrics are held in relationship with the accountabilities in life. For individuals, the ever-expanding circle may include coworkers, family, or friends who are invited to experience the value of metrics that offer meaning to all.

This field guide is a strategy for congregational leaders to successfully develop meaningful metrics. The metrics are not an end in themselves. They are only one way to calibrate ministry in a changing world with a focus on discipleship as God's story is told and retold in an expanding, outward-focused ministry.

Overview

This resource will bring together theological thinking, proven social science models, and organizational practices to help congregational leaders put a plan in place for identifying and using faithful metrics.

Think of this as a field guide designed for a particular type of congregational leader. People who self-identify as pilgrims and are on their own spiritual journey with a yearning to feel the Holy Spirit burning in their hearts. People who are not satisfied with just going through the motions of personal or church life.

These are people who embody a pilgrim spirituality.

This is not a field guide for people who are looking for a quick fix that will make serving in congregational leadership easier. Instead, this field guide offers a process that will illuminate values, set faithful metrics that drive mission, and has the potential to shift behaviors over time.

Each section in the field guide is purposeful and is most effective when done in the order in which it is presented. Skipping ahead to create a congregational dashboard, to track progress, without identifying values and setting clear goals may provide some information, but taking the time to build a solid foundation will lead to greater meaning and better decisions in the long run.

The Camino de Santiago will serve as a metaphor for the journey through this field guide. The Camino de Santiago is a network of paths leading to the shrine of the apostle

Saint James the Great located in the Cathedral of Santiago de Compostela in Galicia, Spain. Tradition has it that the remains of the saint are buried there. Many pilgrims from across the world follow its routes as a way to grow a deeper spirituality.

The intent of this metaphor is to provide a rhythm of faith practices, information, and exercises as a resource for disciples. This field guide encourages practices similar to those of a pilgrimage: Leaders prayerfully listen to God as they ask new questions about life and ministry.

As people of faith, we do not compartmentalize our lives. Rather we integrate our faith practices, our mindset, our theological lens, and our physical activity for a holistic approach to being God's people. We live each day as disciples, regardless of what the day brings. Jesus modeled this as he talked about the kingdom of God, fed people, and went away to pray. All are part of a faithful life.

It is LEAD's hope that you, the reader, will use the stories of the Camino to create your own pattern of prayer, thought, action, and reflection.

A way through the fog for leaders

While walking the Camino de Santiago, an ancient spiritual pilgrimage, we learned three things that are helpful to leaders searching for metrics in a changing world:
⊕ Pay attention to the hot spots
⊕ Stories shape culture
⊕ God is full of surprises

Each of these ideas will frame one section in this field guide, markers that shape the path forward as we share what LEAD has learned about the use of metrics by people of faith.

LEAD is committed to metrics that drive mission, deepen discipleship, and help leaders make decisions about whether to pivot or persevere.

God's people can find significant measures implicit in the Biblical narratives. Without an explicit framework to reveal these metrics, however, some might assume that it is unfaithful, or at least less faithful, to pay attention to these markers. Others may over-focus on a few metrics that can derail mission. The question, "What does success look like?" is a challenging one for a church.

Walking the Camino de Santiago in Spain

So you've never been to Spain?

Go ahead and channel (or Google) the old Three Dog Night song, *"Well, I've never been to Spain, but I kinda like the music..."* for a minute to feel the groove. LEAD is inviting you to enter into your own Camino as you journey through this field guide, so don't let geography trip you up.

If you are seeking new paths for measuring congregational ministry, join LEAD on this journey, opening your heart and mind to the metaphor of the Camino.

Imagine a dirt path through the open countryside with farmland beyond the trees. Imagine as you walk under the trees lining the road, with the sun shining through to create remarkable patterns of light and darkness, that you are walking on stained glass windows.

Imagine walking by small towns with ancient stone buildings lining narrow paths and painted yellow arrows leading the way. Imagine large cities with busy, noisy traffic.

Imagine beautiful Spain with people from all over the world walking. Literally thousands of pilgrims from across the world, all making their way to the same destination as local people go about their normal daily lives farming, doing business, going to school, cleaning house, etc.

Imagine walking and stepping aside for people running past, groups riding bicycles, or others pushing an occupied wheelchair or carrying a child.

While some people walk for months, the LEAD group took the shorter Camino, the final 100 kilometers (roughly 80 miles) in seven days.

Each pilgrim walked for their own reason even if, as is often the case on the Camino, the reason they started didn't end up being the ultimate reason at all. This is the nature of pilgrimage. The surprises on the journey, both good and bad, affect the experience.

The Camino is a journey to a holy place with an awareness that the holy is already happening within and among those on the journey.

The LEAD story, as it unfolds in this field guide, is only a small snapshot of what it means to live as pilgrims—both on the Camino and beyond. This is an invitation to reflect and to grow your own faith imagination as a pilgrim while you seek to identify metrics for measuring ministry without missing the moments.

The good news is that pilgrimages happen in many ways. On the one hand, living each day as pilgrims creates an openness to encountering God in the midst of daily life. On the other hand, making a healthy choice to get outside of the grind of daily life to create room for sacred space is every bit as much a pilgrimage. At LEAD, we recommend both because the second gives perspective to the first. Stepping away from the responsibilities of daily life to experience liminal space provides a frame for interpreting the mundane as meaningful.

Measuring ministry, moments, and impact

This field guide pulls together the gathering of data and Christian leadership. Measuring ministry, moments, and impact is a lot like the concepts revealed on a pilgrimage that offer:

⊕ Deeper understanding of Christian ministry (diakonia) as service among others. This includes responsibility for liturgical and sacramental leadership as well as acts of compassion, justice, and healing done in the name of Christ through the power of the Holy Spirit.

⊕ Clearer understanding of sacred moments as meaningful encounters with the Holy Spirit, often in relationship with others even strangers.

⊕ Broader understanding of the impact of what God is doing in our lives and in the world around us.

Measuring ministry, moments, and impact has greater meaning if you are personally growing through this journey. As a pilgrim, expanding your mindset and bringing new questions to your own leadership may be more important than what happens in any set of metrics. *Faithful Metrics* offers a Learn-Reflect-Act rhythm in each of the three sections on ministry, moments, and impact.

Learn

Learning, or being reminded of what is already known, provides the opportunity to think deeply about ministry. Each learner starts in a different place depending on their own journey. The hope of this field guide is that the very activities of determining and setting metrics, and using what is discovered to influence ministry, will bring a new vision for the sacred.

Reflect

This kind of learning begs space for personal and shared reflection. Reflecting claims the struggle of liminal space. The hope is that

metrics will include both technical and adaptive perspectives. By really wrestling to create the best set of metrics, even tweaking them once they are set if a more faithful approach is discerned, the congregation will have a meaningful ministry gauge rather than a checklist of things to get done. In other words, the holy work of setting metrics for a faith community must include digging into the heart of faith itself.

Act

These kinds of metrics call people to action. By leading out of what is learned and reflected upon, actions will indeed have greater impact. Acting out of metrics includes engaging the larger community as metrics move beyond the leadership table. It is not enough for a few to own and benefit from this experience. For metrics to embody any real revitalization movement, they must be experienced by a critical mass of people who will make the new learning, new reflection, and new action truly transformational. Each chapter assumes the work from the previous chapter has been done. It is recommended to be work shared by a core team of people from the council or another leadership group. The rhythm of learning, reflecting, and acting is circular. What feels like the last act offers a new learning and a new opportunity for reflection.

Learn-Reflect-Act Model for Creating a Movement

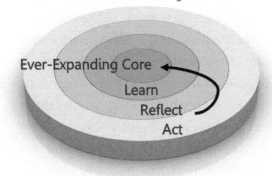

Embracing and expanding diversity

This design, with the intentional rhythm of Learn-Reflect-Act, brings more and more people into the core with each section of this field guide inviting new people in the community to be transformed and transforming. In doing so, expanding circles of people are engaged in making meaning out of their own faith pilgrimage as metrics are determined, interpreted, and lived out in daily life.

Imagine concentric circles where the center of the circle expands. The role of the core team becomes increasingly important as they manage both the process and a movement simultaneously.

Given this rhythm, it is not surprising that leaders on the core team using this process in a faith community will quickly discover that everyone in the group has a different perspective. There are countless ways that individual journeys intersect in a movement like this.

Diversity of gifts

People's past experience with life, their pain and joy, faith and leadership, all come with them to the leadership table and influence their perspective. Fast-thinking decision-makers can easily lose patience with the more process-oriented people or the contemplative personalities in the mix. Meanwhile, the more process-oriented people or more reflective people may shut down if the decision-makers dominate.

This field guide values all learning styles, gifts, and stages of learning as crucial to the richness of the community. Discounting the gifts, joys, pains, and heartaches of others misses the most important component of Christian community. As people who are aware of God's unconditional grace poured into their lives, the community that bears Christ's name is called to be a place of grace and forgiveness.

The Learn-Reflect-Act model of this field guide is designed to engage people from all perspectives. Even more importantly, it is designed to invite leaders out of their comfort zone to nurture a deeper faith while leading an ever-growing, inclusive community.

Diversity is central to the art of Christian leadership and requires negotiating all the nuances of humanity that may be present in any given community.

LEAD is well aware of the power dynamics that exist in every faith community. Faithful leadership takes seriously the need to manage the power dynamic on behalf of those most vulnerable, the poor, the marginalized, the very young, and the very old. It also recognizes an imperative that those in power extend power to the non-majority ethnic, socioeconomic, sexuality, or gender groups in the community. The metrics that are set can create space for a community that is committed to loving God and neighbor.

Diversity of faith journey

The Camino is a perfect image for both an individual and a communal life of faith. It represents a microcosm of human diversity. People are exposed to a broader view of the world and of human nature on this ancient road than they are in most congregations. Yet your congregation (or your family, coworkers, and friends) is more interesting than you probably imagine. Each person you know is on their own pilgrimage, shaped by their own life story. All have blind spots and struggle with the bias that others think like they do. But they don't.

Faithful metrics are designed to encourage movement that nurtures a deeper faith. As metrics are established, an open mindset is key for interpreting meaning.

A quick introduction to adult leadership agility is helpful for setting metrics that measure more than technical, logistical data. The goal of this field guide is to spark

imagination about discipleship, to include metrics that dare to put the sacred on a dashboard because it is so important.

Most congregations are reluctant to expect adults to commit to intentional learning ministries, faith practices, or leadership development. Instead, they invest in the faith formation of children, although this effort is also weakening. By investing only in faith formation of children, congregations miss the opportunity to grow faith and spirituality in adults.

Setting faithful metrics can create a new faith imagination and begin to influence a different outcome in the formation of Christian leaders.

Almost 40 years of research has shown that faith is caught from person to person, most often in the home from parents, grandparents, and other caring adults. Roland Martinson, in his book *The Spirit of Youth and Culture of Youth Ministry: Leading Congregations Toward Exemplary Youth Ministry,* makes it clear that the role of the adult is primary. Vital adult faith, then, is at the heart of the faith of our children. It is also critical to the capacity of Christian leaders to create a faith community that does more than follow good order. To be more like Jesus, to follow the Holy Spirit into the future, and to receive the grace of a loving God, adults must deepen their own discipleship.

Most leaders in congregations aren't satisfied with their own faith practices, much less the current state of the adult learners around them. Even so, little is done in the local congregation to raise the bar. Paying attention to the full spectrum of adult learners provides opportunities for setting more effective faithful metrics.

Diversity of leadership agility

In their book, *Leadership Agility: Five Levels of Mastery for Anticipating and Initiating Change*, Bill Joiner and Stephen Josephs identify what they call "levels of agility" for adult learners. Their work builds on research from the 1950s by psychologists, including Jean Piaget and Erik Erikson, to map the stages through which infants evolve into adults.

In the early 1980s, a series of academic studies identified significant correlations between what happens to people as they grow from stage to stage and how leaders become more effective. Researchers whose work informs LEAD's thinking include William R. Torbert, author of *Action Inquiry: The Secret of Timely and Transforming Leadership* and other books; Robert Kegan, author of *The Evolving Self* and *In Over Our Heads: The Mental Demands of Modern Life*; Don Beck and Chris Cowan, authors of *Spiral Dynamics;* and Ken Wilber, author of over a dozen books based on the stage development framework. They discovered that as people grow from one stage to another, there are distinct sets of mental and emotional capacities that enable people to respond more effectively to change and complexity. By increasing their resiliency and

ability to respond to change, people become more effective.

The Levels of Agility chart (on page 20) provides some perspective on adults both in the church and in the community. Notice the percentages for each level of agility in the chart. Leadership agility is correlated with the capacity for adaptive leadership.

LEAD is making a small bet that leadership in the church mirrors the research by Joiner and Josephs. If that is true, about 80% of congregational leaders can be categorized as Heroic, as people who assume sole responsibility for setting objectives and for coordinating and managing the activities of others. Joiner and Josephs break Heroic leaders down further into two groups intended to emphasize their strengths:
⊕   Experts who are likely to be skilled in particular subject-matter areas
⊕   Achievers who are highly motivated to accomplish outcomes based on their values.

These leaders can be highly effective in certain situations, especially in the work of technical leadership.

Ten percent or less of congregational leaders are Post-Heroic. These are the leaders who work to create highly participatory teams and congregations with shared commitment and responsibilities. As the world constantly changes, becoming more and more complex, it is those who are committed to developing genuinely collaborative teams and congregations with a deep sense of shared purpose who will be able to provide the adaptive leadership needed in the future.

Minimal metrics, maximum movement

Faithful metrics encourage agency with an expectation that God will use God's people in surprising ways to build up the community of believers. This includes the ability to notice when people are not using their gifts and passions or when their agendas and self-interest are at risk of derailing the mission. Faithful metrics also call individuals to personal accountability when their own needs are in conflict with the needs of the whole. Self-awareness is part of the journey. Disciples will always face these personal tensions as they and the ministry grow.

This a starting place. Sadly, the spark of curiosity needed to ignite deeper discipleship is barely burning in most congregations. When it does begin to grow, the results are powerful.

Transformational adult discipleship does exist. It can be seen when leaders discover a breakthrough response to an existing reality as they hear God calling the church out of itself.

LEAD has story after story of what happens when a congregation understands that their needs are part of the mix, but not the whole agenda of the congregation. This happens when people are growing in their faith. Stories of these revitalizing congregations are available at waytolead.org/metrics. Email lead@waytolead.org to add your story to this travelogue.

Looking at the Levels of Agility Chart again, imagine you were creating a similar chart that would deepen the faith life of your people, starting where they are right now.

LEAD offers the idea of setting faithful metrics as one way to engage both technical (usually Heroic) and adaptive (usually Post-Heroic) congregational leaders in the conversation. LEAD believes that every congregation can grow, but growth is a choice. It is a choice that begins with leaders who are willing to engage in their own transformation. The hope is that as faith of the leaders deepens, the congregation will be revitalized.

Agility and discipleship

The left two columns of the chart below offer a snapshot of the Levels of Agility by Joiner and Josephs. The right column is LEAD's application of this research to Christian leadership. LEAD values building our best thinking on solid social science research.

This chart offers an opportunity for rich conversation as congregational leaders examine faith practices with a commitment to engaging people at all levels of agility. The church is unique as it is one of the few places in society that gathers five generations and welcomes every aspect of diversity as an expression of God's grace.

Level of Agility	View of Leadership by Joiner and Josephs	Discipleship Model by LEAD
Heroic Leadership	**Solo leadership solves problems for others**	**Shared values and goals**
Expert (~45%)	Tactical, problem-solving orientation. Believes that leaders are respected and followed by others because of their authority and expertise.	Using lead metrics to deepen values and live out goals.
Achiever (~35%)	Strategic outcome orientation. Believes that leaders motivate others by making it challenging and satisfying to contribute to larger objectives.	Practicing by leading collaborative experiments.
Post-Heroic Leadership	**Collaborative leaders discover and create new solutions**	**God moments shared in relationships and stories**
Catalyst (~5%)	Visionary, facilitative orientation. Believes that leaders articulate an innovative, inspiring vision and bring together the right people to transform the vision into reality. Leaders empower others and actively facilitate their development.	Reflecting on a growing awareness of God moving in, through, and ahead of us as a church.
Co-creator (~4%)	Oriented towards shared purpose and collaboration. Believes leadership is ultimately a service to others. Leaders collaborate with other leaders to develop a shared vision that each experiences as deeply purposeful.	Creating a culture of discipleship with outward movement.
Synergist (~1%)	Holistic orientation. Experiences leadership as participation in a palpable life purpose that benefits others while serving as a vehicle for personal transformation.	Knowing everything intersects with God.

Note: Pre-expert (~10%) is not shown in this chart

How to use this field guide

This field guide is written for Christians to use at their leadership tables. There are three sections that can be navigated during a retreat or over several months. Sample designs for using this field guide are available at waytolead.org/metrics.

Each section includes three chapters. The sequence of these sections is intentional. If the congregation already has shared core values and a clear purpose, starting with Section 2 is an option. This is a journey creating outward-facing adaptive goals with both lag and lead metrics interpreted through stories. The journey is never over, as with time, the metrics will inform goals and influence values and purpose.

The metaphor of the Camino de Santiago is helpful as leaders prayerfully discern Faithful Metrics for their ministry. Congregational life is filled with opportunities and challenges that make a linear process problematic. The gift of the Camino is the constant awareness that God is up to something in the midst of the highs and lows of life. Distractions, detours, and obstacles along the way may be perfect opportunities to recalibrate with renewed awareness of God moving through our lives.

Pilgrimage is more about the journey than the destination. So it is with Faithful Metrics.

Measuring ministry without missing the moments:

This is a map of your journey through this field guide. Just as each person's journey on the Camino is unique, your journey will be unique. The map shows you the path and identifies milestones, yet allows you space to stop and catch your breath or to get back on track if you've lost your way. *Faithful Metrics* is divided into three sections, each with three chapters. Take time along the way to rest and reflect. It could be that the journey itself is the destination.

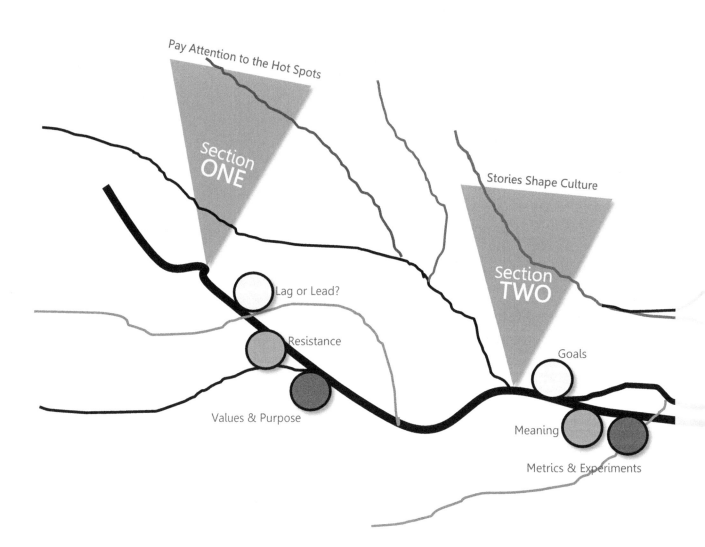

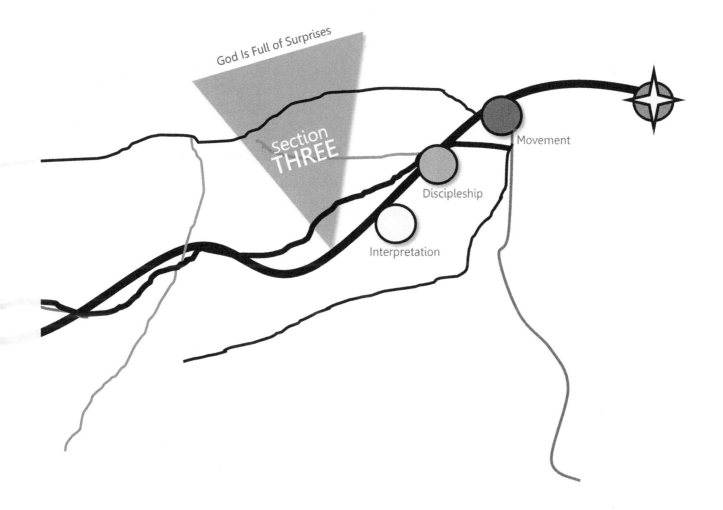

God Is Full of Surprises

Section
THREE

Movement

Discipleship

Interpretation

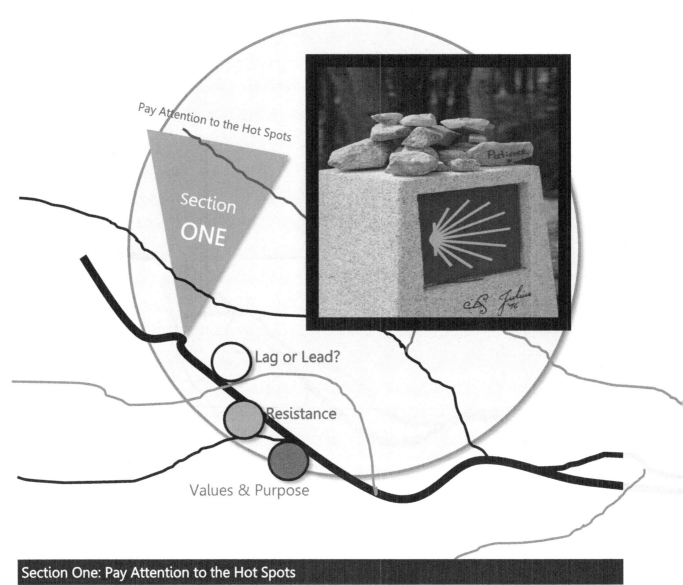

Section One: Pay Attention to the Hot Spots

Chapter 1. Lag or Lead?—What does your congregation measure?
   Learn to identify both kinds of metrics

Chapter 2. Resistance—Why is there reluctance to use metrics if they are not new to the church?
   Reflect on our collective struggle with metrics

Chapter 3. Values and Purpose—How do they increase the power of faithful metrics?
   Act together to identify shared values

Section One: Pay Attention to the Hot Spots

Warning signs

Before starting to walk the Camino, seasoned walkers warned us about hot spots. In all honesty, most of us just smiled and nodded, not really understanding what they were talking about. By the third day, however, everyone knew exactly what they meant.

It turns out that the body gives a little warning right before getting a blister. No kidding. You get a hot spot. Generally speaking, pilgrims have less than fifteen minutes before their skin moves from hot and red to blistered. In that brief period, there is a choice to make:

Pay attention to the hot spot or ignore the warning sign.

By simply stopping to sit down, take off your shoes, cool your feet, and, if possible, put on clean(ish) socks, all will be well. It only takes a little time and attention. But ignore the warning signs and the rest is history.

Connect this to the church. Ask yourself, "Where are the hot spots?"

Over the past 20 years or more, there have been multiple warning signs in the church that leaders have ignored. The research has been broadcast without influence. The sad but true evidence is in plain sight, yet the church has kept walking as if everything was OK The effort needed to keep the "church machine" oiled and moving is exhausting and has distracted leaders from the hot spots in ways that cannot be denied.

Here are a few examples of hot spots that LEAD has heard about from leaders speaking with heartfelt grief or even, on occasion, shame and blame:

⊕ I remember when we wanted to build this building because we were bursting at the seams. Today the mortgage is killing us and the space sits empty most of the week.

⊕ I remember when parents used to bring their children to Sunday School. These classrooms were packed with little ones. Today a few parents will drop their children off, but most don't bother to get up on Sunday morning. If they would only bring their children, all would be well.

⊕ I remember when there were people who felt honored to be on church council. Today we can barely get enough people to serve and too often we end up recycling the same people over and over.

⊕ I remember when we had big confirmation classes. True, most didn't stay, but at least they were confirmed.

You get the drift.

What hot spots have you seen in your congregation? What's on your list?

Many of the Band-Aids that have been carefully applied to cover up or ignore the painful hot spots have fallen off, revealing blisters that might look like changing staff, adding programs, or writing mission statements. Leaders are tired and out of breath.

Coming to terms with hot spots is part of the way forward. In the spirit of author and researcher Brené Brown, from her book *Rising Strong,* leaders need to have both a reckoning and a rumble to find the truth—and a way forward.

First the reckoning, a word that means to narrate or make an account. Engaging with feelings and getting curious about the story behind the feelings are part of the reckoning. "You either walk into your story and own your truth, or you live outside of your story, hustling for your worthiness," Brown writes. (p. 45)

Without this time of accounting to recognize feelings about hot spots, it is too easy to become nostalgic. Romanticizing the good old days lets people tell lies about the hot spots. A time of reckoning names the painful truth about the decline. It has not happened overnight. The church has just been busy, very busy, asking the wrong questions.

Then comes the rumble. This means getting honest about your part in ignoring the hot spots. The rumble starts when leaders have the willingness, ability, and courage to admit that this is their watch, and they have had a part in creating the problem. Then can hopefully be part of the cure.

The nostalgic stories people love to tell about the past are clogging leaders' vision for the church of the future. They are stopping leaders from being honest about the hot spots. This is normal. But these stories will not help them move forward. They are just more Band-Aids.

Brown says that:

> In the absence of data, we will always make up stories. It's how we are wired. In fact, the need to make up a story, especially when we are hurt, is part of our most primitive survival wiring. Making meaning is in our biology, and our default is often to come up with a story that makes sense, feels familiar, and offers us insight into how best to self-protect. What we're trying to do in the rumble—choosing to feel uncertain and vulnerable as we rumble with the truth—is a conscious choice. A brave, conscious choice. (p. 79)

Ripping off the Band-Aid hurts

Short-term pain equals long-term gain. Or does it? When LEAD is invited to work with congregational leaders, we can see the fear in their eyes. Not just fear because their congregation is in decline, but real anxiety that we will make things worse. This fear grows from years of consultants selling cures to what ails the church, only to create division and new pain.

This palpable fear of how people from the outside will mess up the congregation is seen in defensive postures and closed mindsets. While experts can warm people up over time, what would happen if the existing leaders in the congregation were coached? What if the leaders worked their own problems?

LEAD's work is to grow leaders who lead their own congregations. Our focus is not to show up as the experts but to accompany people so they have the courage to live out their God-given call to serve, love, and lead.

Leave the Band-Aid on the hot spot for a few more minutes while you fall in love with a God who forgives and loves you for being human. Feel the grace. Then local leaders can ease the hot spot into the warm waters of Baptism and the Band-Aids will loosen on their own.

Facing hot spots calls for some confession of sin. There is no place in the church for hot spots such as racism, sexism, genderism, etc. It is the call of the church to get out of its

own way so that the church can truly point to a healing, loving God.

Ripping off the Band-Aid is best done one step at a time. To be sure, some bleeding is necessary. But starting with love is the right first step. When leaders love their people, their people know it. It is these leaders, leaders that they trust, whom they will follow. Leadership 101 has said this for years, but the impatience to move the church forward has made hot spots into serious infections. The only way around this is to really love the people God has given you to lead, even if you don't always like them.

Leaders are not always that lovable either. It's good to start with humility and an awareness of your own growing edges. Let's face it, if leaders knew exactly what to do, they would already be doing it.

Healing from hot spots

Many of the deeper pains felt in the church serve as important reminders that the church does not live in isolation apart from the larger society. The shifts in the world are happening fast. Leaders can easily turn inward as the church declines. This inward focus will bury the church. It is much healthier and more hopeful to turn outward into the neighborhood and larger world.

For the church to have a future and for metrics to be helpful at all, the leadership of the church must look beyond the current people in worship with an imagination for a more diverse population. They must envision a new church. Creating an outward movement starts with a true desire by leaders to embrace the greatest commandment:

"The first is, 'Hear, O Israel: the Lord our God, the Lord is one; you shall love the Lord your God with all your heart, and with all your soul, and with all your mind, and with all your strength.' The second is this, 'You shall love your neighbor as yourself.' There is no other commandment greater than these." Mark 12:29-31

Leaders and faith communities across the globe fall short of these commandments as their humanity gets in the way. At its core, the church is a gathering place for broken people. People living with, tending, or ignoring hot spots day and night.

The church is perfect for this kind of problem. Confession is central to Christian life. It is an acknowledgement that everyone has fallen short by what has been done or left undone. In confession, the church acknowledges that people are not God. Through confession, the church believes that people, and communities of people, can be healed, freed from suffering and death for an abundant life.

Leaders who confess and are forgiven create space for trying new ways of being church. Loving the past and experimenting into the future must be held together at the same time. The rich heritage of the church means always sorting out what will be kept while opening our eyes and our doors to new cultures, generations, ethnicities, and other forms of diversity. The church is freed to try again because it is forgiven.

Pause for prayers of healing...

Pause to inhale the grace of God and exhale your fears, stress, and exhaustion when you see each shell stamp at the start of a new chapter. **Now, together we pray:**

For self-centered living, and for failing to walk with humility and gentleness:
Holy God, holy and might, holy and immortal, have mercy on us.

For misuse of human relationships, and for unwillingness to see the image of God in others:
Holy God, holy and mighty, holy and immortal, have mercy on us.
—*Evangelical Lutheran Worship, p. 240*

1. Lag or Lead?

What does your congregation measure?

Text Message: How about a cup of coffee?
Me: OOOOOKAAAYYYY... why?

Text Message: To pick your brain about your small group. What is working so that the same people are still coming after four years? What curriculum do you use?
Me: Why?

Text Message: Our metrics tell us that people are coming, some are joining but they don't stay.
Me: Wait—you have metrics that tell you this?

Text Message: Yes.
Me: Let's meet tomorrow. (Spoiler alert, it's not about a perfect curriculum, it's about relationships.)

For transparency, this conversation doesn't happen every day—but it did really happen. Faith Lutheran Church in Bellaire, Texas, has weekly, monthly, and annual metrics that are driving their questions. Staff review these like clockwork. Samples of dashboards are available at waytolead.org/metrics.

A dashboard provides a way to compare metrics over time. This is a progress report to collect data, that provides a snapshot of your ministry.

Typical congregational metrics, including attendance at worship and weekly offering totals, provide some information about reality. At best, they paint a picture of where things are right now. But there is a lot more to the story that really matters and these metrics aren't getting there.

By charting these same numbers over time, trends emerge. The trends themselves impact confidence and may even be used to cast future direction. This is sobering news considering the decline in numbers of both people and giving within mainline Christian churches in the United States.

Still, these numbers tell some hard truth. Or at least they tell a part of the truth. The number of people in attendance is absolutely an indicator of *something* since we know people vote with their feet. Not showing up for worship or other religious programming is a story worth investigating with genuine curiosity and an openness to use what is learned to transform ministry. A real reckoning (account) and rumble (owning the stories you are making up) is part of the healing process.

The church could benefit from more of this to keep nostalgia in perspective.

Sadly, leaders are more likely to see the typical congregational metrics of noses and nickels, setting off a chain of unhelpful reactions. Declining numbers of people in worship may give way to leaders rethinking worship styles without doing any homework to find out why people don't come or why they left. The automatic response is often "we need different music" or some other quick fix.

The real answer is: Maybe. Or maybe not. There is to know why people aren't coming unless someone asks them.

Even more troubling is when leaders use these metrics to blame others for the decline. "If only our pastor, or our organist, or our children's programs... were like X church."

This is not helpful.

To borrow a concept from Marilee Adams[1], too often the impulse is to move into a Judger, rather than a Learner, Mindset. She points out that blame keeps people stuck in the past while responsibility paves the way for a better future. Owning the fact that the current congregational system is producing exactly what it was designed to create is a good place to start.

Over-focus on typical congregational metrics, like "butts and bucks," works against congregational vitality and a vision of a hopeful future. Leaders experience growing feelings of hopelessness and avoid trying new things because they fear making things worse.

Just because an annual reporting system calls for an accounting of attendance and assets doesn't mean they are the only metrics that matter. Who or what is stopping leaders from expanding the reporting to get a bigger view of reality?

When caring people feel cornered by data that they take personally, one natural response is to circle the wagons. Let's face it, there is a lot that leaders cannot control. Feeling out of control can paralyze even the strongest leader. But leaders *can* choose the questions they ask. There *are* choices.

Leaders can and should change what is measured. Numbers of people in worship and money in the offering plate are lag metrics. (This is a common key performance indicator in the sales and social science worlds.)

A lag metric is something that has already happened by the time you get the data.

At this point, there is nothing you can do to change the outcome because the information provided comes too late.

Noses and nickels are great examples. By the time you count how many people are in church or how much money they give, the numbers are what they are.

Focusing on lag metrics[2] weakens leadership's ability to make change. Lag

---

Learn more: [1]Marilee Adams, *Change Your Questions, Change Your Life: 10 Powerful Tools for Life and Work*
[2]Chris McChesney, Sean Covey, and Jim Huling, *The 4 Disciplines of Execution: Achieving Your Wildly Important Goals* provides more information on these lag-lead metrics.

metrics can be discouraging and create feelings of powerlessness.

Even worse, over-focus on lag metrics tends to move leaders toward feelings of guilt, low self-worth, and failure. For leaders prone to problem-solving, lag metrics may kick them into high gear as they frantically up their game, imagining growth will come at the end of a long list of programs that exhaust everyone involved.

Or for those who are competitive, the response to these lag metrics may look a lot like lying. Many leaders will admit that their numbers of people in worship are inflated because of a reluctance to share honest data. This is a common response to the current paradigm of success. Manipulating numbers, especially around attendance, to avoid looking bad may lead congregations to include everyone who shows up to their building on a Sunday in their worship metric, even those who are there for meetings, 12-step groups, or Scout troops.

These lag metrics undermine integrity and cause leaders to lose their confidence and their focus on God's mission. This negative accountability reinforces unhelpful behavior. It's a losing proposition for hard-working staff and volunteers.

It is worth repeating: By the time a lag metric is recorded, nothing can be done to change the outcome. Nothing, that is, except to lie. Lead metrics, on the other hand, are predictive and can be influenced.

Lead metrics are the indicators that leaders strategically set and that have the potential for changing the lag metric.

> **Metrics are not a new idea...**
>
> Day by day, as they spent much time together in the temple, they broke bread at home and ate their food with glad and generous hearts, praising God and having the goodwill of all the people.
>
> And day by day the Lord added to their number those who were being saved.
> *Acts 2:46-48*

For example:

⊕ What is the one thing the church is going to do on a Sunday morning to make visitors feel welcome?

⊕ How often? Who? When? Why?

⊕ How many times in the course of a year does the church equip, inspire, and support people to share their faith story?

⊕ Who? When? How often?

⊕ How much money and time is given each month by people in worship to reduce human need in the local neighborhood?

A lead metric will always lead somewhere.

Lead metrics are incremental indicators, like a hope-filled formula that reads:

If you do more of X, you will see Y result.

Of course, the opposite can also be true: If you do less of X, you will see less of Y.

Identifying lead metrics is hard. People are wired to default to lag metrics; even LEAD wrestles with this. It takes intentionality to go after this new framework to name, test, and finally adopt specific, measurable lead metrics.

An example may be helpful. Think about taking a course at school. Your grade at the end of the semester is a lag metric. Once the semester is over and your grade has been entered, there is nothing you can do to change it. The monthly, weekly, and daily work you do (attending class, completing assignments, and taking quizzes) are all lead metrics. They provide you with information along the way and an opportunity to change the lag metric before it's too late.

Another more personal example expands this understanding of lag and lead metrics. People place high value on good health, but health can be difficult to measure. One common metric is weight, but, as with worship attendance, the number you see when you step on the scale (or on Monday morning when you total all the worship figures) is what it is. You can't go back in time and change course to get a different result. That's because weight and worship attendance are both lag metrics. Continuing to count these lag metrics does not move you (or the congregation) forward. Merely tallying these numbers week after week will not make you more healthy or move your congregation toward deeper discipleship.

Weight and attendance do not tell the whole story, and the story they do tell may not even be the right one.

To make change, real change, happen, the focus needs to be on lead metrics. By paying attention to the lead metrics, people can shift behaviors to produce different outcomes.

Returning to the example of health, increasing activity, as measured by steps on a Fitbit, could be one lead metric. Working toward a specific number of steps each day can influence the number on the scale (or another lag metric like blood pressure or BMI) and help a person achieve the goal of a healthy lifestyle.

Now, think about church attendance again. What are lead metrics that will move the congregation toward deeper discipleship? What lag metrics might help you see if you get there?

This isn't easy, but it is worth the effort. In the end, it is the only way to use metrics to create the kind of momentum leaders are looking for as they join in God's mission.

You can find examples of lag-lead metrics everywhere, even in scripture. Jesus' teachings offer many illustrations of how faith practices inspire faith lives. Using the lag-lead lens allows you to read your beloved Bible stories with new eyes.

Take any text and ask yourself, is there a lead or lag metric being communicated here?

Or use this outline for personal reflection and a group conversation.

Bible conversation

Read Luke 10:25-37, the Good Samaritan story. Now ask yourself, what are the lag (in the past, only recording what has happened) or lead (in the future, can influence change) metrics in this story?

Circle your answer. Discuss this with others.

1. "Teacher," he said, "what must I do to inherit eternal life?" **lag or lead**
2. "What is written in the law? What do you read there?" **lag or lead**
3. He answered, "You shall love the Lord your God with all your heart, and with all your soul, and with all your strength, and with all your mind; and your neighbor as yourself." And he said to him, "You have given the right answer; do this, and you will live." **lag or lead**
4. But wanting to justify himself, he asked Jesus, "And who is my neighbor?" **lag or lead**
5. "A man was going down from Jerusalem to Jericho, and fell into the hands of robbers, who stripped him, beat him, and went away, leaving him half dead. Now by chance a priest was going down that road; and when he saw him, he passed by on the other side. So likewise a Levite, when he came to the place and saw him, passed by on the other side. But a Samaritan while traveling came near him; and when he saw him, he was moved with pity. He went to him and bandaged his wounds, having poured oil and wine on them. Then he put him on his own animal, brought him to an inn, and took care of him. The next day he took out two denarii, gave them to the innkeeper, and said, 'Take care of him; and when I come back, I will repay you whatever more you spend.' Which of these three, do you think, was a neighbor to the man who fell into the hands of the robbers?" **lag or lead**

Did you notice how Jesus takes the question in #1 and responds with a story, #5? Can you see how #2 points to a particular interpretation of the law as a lag? More on stories as metrics in the next section.

Your thoughts?

The LEAD team's responses are: 1. lag, 2. lag, 3. lead, 4. lag, 5. lead. Do you agree or disagree?

By now you are probably shaking your head and thinking, "Where is this going?" or "How can we possibly come up with the right metrics?" These are great questions that will be discussed in the chapters ahead.

The first step is to clearly understand the difference between lag and lead. Behavior always produces something. Even little things have impact over time. This is true for you personally and certainly true for the church.

Faithful Metrics is an invitation to measure behaviors that are lead metrics, especially those with the potential to shift the lag metric of deepened discipleship. A good starting place is to understand that what you measure influences what you produce. Here are some examples of personal lag and lead metrics to consider:

Lag metric: Deeper faith life

Some possible lead metrics that help you achieve your lag metric:

⊕ Pray a mealtime grace at every meal
⊕ Journal "God moments" from your day
⊕ Share a meal or cup of coffee with someone you don't know very well
⊕ Increase generosity by sharing money or other gifts that are unexpected
⊕ Walk a labyrinth, Stations of the Cross, or other active prayer practice
⊕ Worship God in a new way by visiting a church that speaks a different language
⊕ Join or start a small group Bible study
⊕ Commit to a Lenten or Advent practice
⊕ Try a new prayer practice like Centering Prayer or Lectio Divina
⊕ Sign up for digital daily devotions

For more ideas, go to waytolead.org/spiritual-practices/

Lag metric: Better relationships

Some possible lead metrics that help you achieve your lag metric:

⊕ Check in with a special person in your life each week
⊕ Send unexpected thank you notes
⊕ Spend one-on-one time with a child, a partner, or an old friend each month
⊕ Apologize first
⊕ Put all devices down at mealtime

Lag metric: Good health

Some possible lead metrics that help you achieve your lag metric:

⊕ Get an annual physical
⊕ See the dentist and/or eye doctor regularly
⊕ Walk 20 minutes per day
⊕ Limit dessert, wine, or other treats to once or twice a week
⊕ Check the calorie counts at restaurants you frequent to make good choices
⊕ Ask for a to-go box and split your meal before you start to eat

You get the idea. By measuring these small steps (lead metrics), changes can occur. This same approach can work in your family and in your congregation.

A lead metric that will change ——————▶ a lag metric	

2. Resistance

Moving beyond reluctance to metrics

The idea of measuring something as important to you as your church can create an avalanche of self-doubt, raise theological questions, and create overall awkwardness. The language of success may even feel wrong on many levels.

Before jumping into the deeper pushback that may be experienced when it comes to church metrics, think about the powerful role lead metrics play in changing behavior and producing unexpected positive results in other parts of life.

Let's return to the semester grade illustration of lag and lead metrics. Changing study habits is difficult for people to master on their own. Most students need the support of the people they live with and possibly outside help to change their behavior. Tutors, teachers, mentors, coaches, friends, and family can all make it easier to develop self-discipline. With support, the effort is more likely to create new patterns.

What works is when the new, albeit challenging, behavior changes are rewarded with improved test scores long before they show up on a semester report card. Small wins keep students trying until the effort becomes a habit. Encouragement is huge.

While this idea isn't new, thinking about it in terms of lag and lead metrics may be new to you.

Reinforcing new lead metrics in community makes the desired behavior more likely to stick. Simply put, it is much easier to succeed when the people around you champion your cause. Without a strong network, getting better grades is difficult, maybe even impossible. This is one reason children in households without adults who share the value of learning can benefit from mentoring and coaching.

Another illustration is the desire people have to get organized, be more efficient, or somehow get the most out of the same 24 hours. Are there lead metrics that could be helpful here too? A wide variety of resources are available for managing busy lives, setting priorities, and accomplishing goals. In fact, the many new technologies for staying organized can be part of the distraction. Some people find a way forward that helps them focus and creates new habits, at least for a while, but most will need to renew their commitment to self-discipline from time to time.

Take a minute to reflect on your personal journey through various technologies over the years. As a culture, we have moved from paper calendars or day planners to digital calendars. Now, for the really organized, there are digital project management tools that interface with various other platforms and devices to maximize our organizational pleasure. Whole industries are organized around organizing. How's that going for you?

It is no wonder that there are people who talk about getting organized but never do. In their heart of hearts, they love living life in all its messiness. They may fear that tidying up would limit their creativity or that the constraints of a structured, disciplined lifestyle (metrics or not) might reduce their entrepreneurial or innovative leadership.

Except, in this case, the opposite is true. When people think about creativity, they think about artistic work, unbridled effort that leads to beautiful effect. But if you look deeper, you'll find that some of the most inspiring art forms, such as haikus, sonatas, and religious paintings, are surrounded by constraints. They are beautiful because

creativity triumphed over the rules. Constraints shape and focus problems and provide clear challenges to overcome. Creativity thrives within constraints.[3]

By pushing through to solve these problems and overcome the challenges, amazing insights can occur. It might even be said that to be your best self as a leader, you have to ruthlessly prioritize. Without limitations, clear values, time-boxes, principles, ethics, practices, and rituals, innovation can be a struggle.

What does this have to do with congregational resistance?

It turns out that the tension created by constraints can be life-giving for faith communities as well, even if most leaders would prefer to eliminate anything that may cause conflict. As Edwin Friedman makes clear in his book, *Generations to Generations: Family Process in Church and Synagogue*, there is a difference between process anxiety and content anxiety. Process anxiety is emotional and related to a change in relationships. Content anxiety is about specific events and is often symptomatic.

In LEAD's experience, the resistance to setting lead metrics is related to a change in relationships (process anxiety). Or put more accurately, the anticipated anxiety of a potential change in relationships.

Learn more: [3]For more on creativity and constraint, check out Yahoo CEO Marissa Meyers' YouTube video: *Top 10 Rules for Success*. https://www.youtube.com/watch?v=02zYZ-JB2zQ.

Yes, we are anxious about the possibilities of creating anxiety.

Interestingly enough, LEAD has found that this is a normal kind of anxiety in congregational leaders. Every time the concept of lead metrics is introduced as essential for shifting lag metrics, people agree to the concept and then quickly follow up with stories about who would be offended by this idea in their congregation.

Leading out of a fear of anticipated anxiety is exhausting and feeds an already anxiety-prone system. LEAD has found that moving forward requires both acknowledging the anticipation of anxiety and a willingness to make a healthy investment into deepening relationships with God and each other.

Relationships are the currency congregational leaders need to move ministry forward. Blowing past people to avoid offending them is not wise. Neither is letting the fear of fear stop you from leading your congregation or giving all the power of leadership to those you are afraid to offend. This relational currency is rooted in our faith. The grace that God generously gives you is the grace you want to offer to others. As you will see in the next chapter, clear shared values provide a way to navigate between giving grace and joining God in mission.

The church has been experiencing hot spots that create anxiety and stress in the system for a very long time. The general population's lack of interest in church life as evidenced by aging membership and

decreasing dollars has the temperature ripe for innovation. One approach is to circle the wagons, while another is to open up space for birthing new, interesting ways of being church.

LEAD understands faithful metrics as intentional, generative constraints that can push a congregation to be more creative, more accountable, and more focused. Moving the focus away from the lag metrics that weigh leaders down opens up an encouraging space for nurturing lead metrics. This is especially true when:

1. **The power to set metrics comes from within.** Faithful metrics are not imposed from the outside by a consultant or guru. They are discerned from the inside with prayerful attention to the Holy Spirit calling the congregation out of itself.

   Leaders of a congregation need to set their own metrics. This field guide offers a template for leaders to frame their own dashboard, but that is only a starting place. Sing your own song, write your own music, set your own pace, and measure your own movement—but do it with an outward, listening ear so that you are hearing God's voice louder than your own personal preferences or those of the powers that be.

2. **Pay attention to the resistance.** The combination of passion and blind spots can make you charge ahead when you should stop to listen. Resistance is a constraint to be navigated.

Understanding underlying anxieties is important when creating a learning organization. The first move of a Christian leader is to discover what God is already doing by deeply listening to God in prayer (to become centered), to stakeholders in the congregation (to become aware), and to the neighbors living near the campus (to become wise).

Lead metrics can relieve the pressure many leaders feel to measure up to nearby congregations that seem to have it all together. By creating incremental lead metrics, leaders are working with and in the system rather than against it.

In their book *The Practice of Adaptive Leadership: Tools and Tactics for Changing Your Organization and the World*, Heifetz, Grashow, and Linsky dedicate a section to diagnosing the system. They write about the elegance and tenacity of the status quo that in organizations, like all human systems, is highly complex. The structures, culture, and defaults that define and maintain them are difficult to change. Paying attention to existing decision-making groups, formal or informal, in order to understand where power lies in the community can point to lead metrics that may engender support. Heifetz, et al. write:

Many organizations get trapped by their current ways of doing things, simply because these ways worked in the past. And as tried-and-true patterns of thinking and acting produced success for the organization, they also produced success

for the individuals who embraced those patterns. The people who rose to the top of the organization because of their ability to work with the system as is will have little interest in challenging its structures, culture or defaults. Moving away from what has worked in the past is especially difficult for people in midcareer who have enjoyed considerable professional success. (p. 51-52)

If this sounds like your reality, then you are in good company. Remember how important the support system of champions and encouragers is to the success of a student in taking on new behaviors? This gives insight to the value of engendering support for any new movement—even the movement of setting metrics—before pushing too hard.

Staff resistance

It is important to be proactive in addressing potential staff resistance. This is a new way of thinking, and adding new metrics can create insecurity among staff who may feel they are being judged, even if they are invited to help design the metrics.

Staff have more at stake. They have a higher investment in the congregation's operations and general practices than even the most dedicated volunteer. Faithful volunteer congregational leaders who have been invested in a particular church setting for longer than anyone on the paid staff may struggle to understand this truth. Although the emotional, spiritual, and financial contributions of volunteers are the life-blood of a congregational system, paid staff have an added dynamic. Their livelihood, which may include health insurance and other benefits, can make them more vulnerable to changes than a volunteer. All of this is part of the complexity of a volunteer faith-based organization.

Using Question Thinking can help to ease this anxiety. Moving from a Judger environment to a Learner environment in your thinking and your conversations with staff and other leaders around metrics provides a safe, nonthreatening space for honest discussion. Encouraging Learner questions takes practice. Notice the shift in tone of these questions.

Judger Questions include questions like this:
⊕ Whose fault is it?
⊕ What's wrong with them?
⊕ Why am I failing?
⊕ Why are they so stupid?

Learner Questions are more like this:
⊕ How can I think about this differently?
⊕ What are they thinking and feeling?
⊕ What is possible in this situation?
⊕ What do I really want?
⊕ What do they really want?

Lead metrics can provide a powerful next step in the congregation and at the same time feel like a potential risk to the staff. A reaction that seems out of proportion to the metric may reveal a staff member that is genuinely passionate and dedicated to the mission. On the other hand, it may be a red flag, indicating that a person is either under-

or over-functioning. If it is the latter, setting related metrics might be a way forward. For example, an over-functioning staff member can be supported in setting boundaries by a metric that everyone on the staff schedules time for continuing education and takes all of their allotted vacation each year.

Under-functioning staff may benefit from a new metric that includes regular review of goals and objectives. Having clear metrics that all have agreed to can level the playing field and set reasonable expectations.

There is always the chance that new metrics may identify people who are in the wrong seat on the bus. Roles may need to be changed, people may need to shift responsibilities, or they may need to be invited to leave. This is not about the metrics themselves. Lead metrics only serve as indicators of an opportunity to rethink a staffing situation.

Less is more

Leaders will find greater success by launching a soft start with lead metrics before moving into highly visible, whole-congregation engagement. A small number of lead metrics, data, and shared results will build trust and increase the value of metrics.

The congregation is best served by identifying three or four lead metrics as gauges that will shift their lag metrics. There is evidence that the more metrics a congregation has in place, the less effective they actually are. Selecting key metrics that create energy for a particular season is crucial, especially if using metrics is a new practice.

It also means that the metrics themselves are up for evaluation. The questions asked will shape results. It is quite possible that it will take a little practice to discover the best questions for this time in your congregation's life. A list of metrics to consider and a design for a digital dashboard is offered at waytolead.org/metrics.

Depending on the level of resistance, the leadership history of the staff, and the trust of paid and volunteer leadership, outside support may be helpful. While consultants should not set metrics, they can provide accountability for the process itself. Joining a cohort with other congregations for mutual accountability and learning is another approach that may yield greater success and transformation than going it alone. Without support, the resistance encountered can be wearing on leaders.

Identifying lead metrics

Metrics are most helpful when set within clear values and designed to measure the goals and objectives of the congregation. A fast-track values clarification process is outlined in the next chapter. For now, let's focus on the *who* part of identifying lead metrics.

The power to set metrics

Most congregations have a governing body of some kind. This could be a church council or board of directors with fiduciary responsibility for stewarding finances, staff, and vision. The instinct is for these leadership tables to tackle this work themselves. As noted earlier, metrics are most effective when the people responsible for executing them are part of the conversation. People support what they help create, so if staff or key volunteers are accountable for moving the needle on a particular metric, they need to have a voice in the process.

When it comes to identifying lead metrics, one size does not fit all. The very process of setting metrics can increase trust and bring new insights. Positive results and deeper relationships can also be byproducts.

Taking a break from the day in and day out responsibilities of ministry and personal life to really focus on metrics in a retreat setting is more effective than meeting week after week, an hour or two at a time.

LEAD has discovered most growing congregations actually leave the church campus for a retreat, even if it means just going to someone's home or across town to another church's campus. When church leaders hold an all-day meeting in the same space they typically meet and call it a retreat, it actually works against the intended goals. LEAD highly recommends investing in annual time away to set lead metrics that will shift the lag metrics. This investment in the relational health of leadership is worth the dollars and time required.

In the words of Heifetz, Grashow, and Linsky, "stepping off the dance floor and moving to the balcony" is crucial. The single most important role of the leader is to be able to diagnose the system and, to do that well, leaders need perspective. In the book, *The Practice of Adaptive Leadership: Tools and Tactics for Changing Your Organization and the World*, they point out that while people are in the middle of the action, they have a very small view of the whole picture. In their language, leaders benefit from getting some emotional and physical distance by walking up the stairs to the balcony. The metaphor of the balcony nudges people to seek new emotional and spiritual perspectives as they move away from their usual position on the dance floor.

What does this have to do with managing resistance to metrics?

A core team of people, including a cross-section of those within the system to implement ministry, stepping onto the balcony for perspective will be able to accomplish the two primary goals named at the beginning of this chapter.

1. Identify lead metrics to test.
2. Name the resistance, as they know it, while recognizing there can and will be surprises.

Suggestions for a 24-hour Metrics Retreat are available at waytolead.org/metrics. They include introducing Question Thinking[4], by Marilee Adams; clarifying values; and setting goals.

Use these prompts for your personal reflections or journaling:
⊕ My initial reaction and experience with lag-lead metrics is...
⊕ Bible stories that come to my mind when I think about metrics are...
⊕ I feel like our current metrics inspire/deflate energy for deepening discipleship when...
⊕ My own reluctance to use metrics for measuring congregational mission are...

Use these questions for group conversation:
⊕ What are hot spots we have seen in our congregation that should alert us to a need for change?
⊕ What roadblocks keep us from using these hot spots as places of curiosity and discovery?
⊕ How can a shift from lag to lead metrics help our leadership be more creative and responsive to these hot spots?
⊕ How do you rate the trust level in the congregation on a scale from 1 to 10?
1= low trust
4 = not bad, not great
6 = good enough to consider new ideas
8 = we are ready to experiment
10 = we are innovating together
⊕ What can we do to deepen relationships?
⊕ How can we teach Question Thinking?

Brainstorm the lead metrics you could set to move the needle on your lag metrics.

Learn more: [4]Marilee Adams, *Change Your Questions, Change Your Life: 10 Powerful Tools for Life and Work*

3. Values and Purpose

Start by identifying shared values.

Values may already be painted on the wall or show up in printed material at church. Chances are good that those values were well honed by a thoughtful group of people earlier this year or, more likely, a few years ago. That's great, but it is not what this field guide is about.

Take a minute and think about your cell phone. Ponder your apps. How many of them did you have three years ago? How many that you can't live without now did you even have an imagination for then?

In the fast-changing world of digital everything, it's important to take a values reality check before setting metrics. Values[5] provide a foundation for the goals and metrics that lead people into deeper faith. Even if there are existing values, validating them in conversation through this quick values process will prepare you for the next steps.

The values exercises in this field guide are not designed to produce timeless values or everlasting metrics for lifelong mission. Instead, they provide a read on your congregation's values today that will help you set metrics in response to what the Holy Spirit is doing now.

Think of this in the same way you raise your prayers to God. Most frequent pray-ers will admit that their prayer life has grown over the years. They would tell you that it has

---

Learn more: [5]For a deeper dive into values, check out the Wake Up Process. This 10-step process helps congregations clarify three types of core values: core beliefs, core convictions, and core practices. The Faithful Metrics Values Card Workshop is a great way to fast-track core convictions, but they will not be owned by the community unless the process engages a critical mass of people.

been shaped by life events and has held them through really hard times. They might say that some days they pray alone on a walk or in their car. Other times they cherish the prayers they share with family, children, or coworkers. And there are days, or even longer, where they can't find the space, words, or heart to pray at all. The common thread is that their prayers are real and they are deepening and maturing over time.

In the same way, a congregation's values can be affirmed, tweaked, or altered based on current events, the political climate, changes in the neighborhood, or deepening faith.

Identifying faithful metrics starts with faithful values, values that will mature over time, like your prayer life. What sustains and guides you right now may not be exactly what you need next year. This is not a values-set-in-stone approach, but rather values that are forming like stones in rushing water.

Are you a congregation that prioritizes young families so that all decisions are made by asking the question, how will this support faith in children? Alternatively, is your priority supporting people in recovery so that their meeting space is always held sacred regardless of who else may want to use the room? When there are competing requests for funding or space or staff time, your values will help you prioritize your resources.

The values setting process

The *Faithful Metrics* field guide has a companion set of values cards for

discovering shared values that can be ordered online at waytolead.org. The cards include web resources and ideas for using them with your family, priority partnerships, or church leadership teams.

Go to waytolead.org/metrics for a variety of resources, including an outline for a values workshop. The workshop assumes you have these cards available. If you don't, it is possible to make your own using the instructions on the website.

Before beginning the activities, you will need to identify groups of people in the congregation who care about congregational metrics. Remember to include staff, council, and key leaders. Each group of eight taking part in the exercise will need a set of 50 cards, either the ones available from LEAD or those you have made.

Once you have your values, what's next?

After your values have been clarified or affirmed, they should be shared with the congregation. Here are 10 ways to make sure the whole congregation understands the values and how they influence the life of the congregation:

1. Preach a different value each week.
2. Preach all three to five values in one sermon.
3. Develop a 3- to 5-week Bible study focusing on a different value each week.
4. Create Facebook posts that express each value, taking one each day for a week.

5. Create three to five personal devotions, each focusing on one of the values, for people to use at home. Deliver these digitally or hand out paper copies at worship.
6. Look for music that expresses each of the values. Highlight the value before and/or after singing each song over the next three to five weeks.
7. Create a logo that illustrates these values to use on everything for the next year.
8. Organize the website around these three to five values.
9. Have a photo contest and ask people to post pictures on Facebook that express each value, one per week.
10. Create a bedtime or mealtime ritual using the words from these values.

Notice that none of these require the council or staff to take on more than they are already doing. You can invite people in the congregation to coordinate one of these new ideas. Even the sermons could include interviews or videos related to the values. Giving this work, with clear tasks and deadlines, to a newly formed group involves more people in the process, and they become invested in the results.

It is also worth noting that none of these ideas cost a lot of money or take years to implement.

The website is the one possible exception, depending on the current state of your congregation's website and congregational leadership skills. It is more important than your landscaping. New people will visit your website before they ever drive by the church; it's the front door to your congregation's ministry. But even website improvements can be made for less than $1,000—a worthwhile investment in congregational values.

Why do this?

The values themselves are not the end; they are only one step toward setting faithful metrics. The hope is to find the centeredness that comes out of the alignment of a values-focused ministry.

Shared values have several additional benefits:
⊕ Values can help people who are new to the congregation understand the congregation's priorities.
⊕ Values can be used for decision-making.
⊕ Values can be used to assess and evaluate ministries that may have outlived their purpose.
⊕ Values can guide sermon and study themes.
⊕ Values can frame budgets.
⊕ Values can give form to all congregational communication.

In the end, the more people who understand that the congregation is driven by its values, the greater the likelihood that the metrics created will bring about the hoped-for transformation. With values in place, congregational leadership is ready to articulate its purpose.

Clarifying purpose: Why does the congregation exist?

Congregational purpose answers the question, "Why do we exist in this place, in this day and time?" A clear identity (or purpose) is at the heart of what it means to be centered. This can be difficult in a fast-changing world where it seems identities are being reformed almost daily. What exactly is the role of the Christian church in a post-Christian society? Today's search for identity in congregational life is more similar to the quest of the early church than to anything seen in the last century.

As Zygmunt Bauman observes in *Identity: Conversations with Benedetto Vecchi:*

> 'Identity' is revealed to us only as something to be invented rather than discovered; as a target of effort, 'an objective'; as something one still needs to build from scratch or to choose from alternative offers and then to struggle for. While identities were once acquired by birth into stable communities, for late-modern or postmodern people today they are the product of endless work and anxiety. (p. 16)

In the recent past, really for most of our lives, the Christian church has not bothered much with the question of identity, focusing instead on the needs of its members. The culture of the church provided it with a role in society similar to that of other organizations people might join although it

could be argued that the church was more highly valued by its membership. In most cases mission was not done by the whole church but rather by committees, by groups dedicated to the support of missionaries, or by youth groups on mission trips.

In today's changing world, many congregations find themselves in survival mode. For decades, churches have been hemorrhaging young people who do not return when they have children of their own. You could ask, what contribution or value is added by being part of a congregation that would inspire people to come? Why should people make time in their busy lives to be part of a congregation? Or more directly, as people often ask LEAD, how can we get more youth and young families with children to come? This kind of thinking has led congregations to try one new program after another, leaving the faithful tired and worn out.

Questions like these feel awkward and consumer driven. Regardless of how many new things the church tries, the church's image is declining along with attendance. In fact, the church is losing its identity. This begs a more important question:

Why does the church, or more specifically *your* church, exist at all?

The overarching answer is that the church's purpose is to be a community that participates in God's mission in the world.
God is a missionary God, who sends the church into the world. This understanding

shifts the agency of mission from the church to God. It is God's mission that has a church rather than a church that has a mission. (Van Gelder and Zscheile, *The Missional Church in Perspective: Mapping Trends and Shaping the Conversation*, p. 3)

You can behave your way into a new way of thinking. The motivation for faithful metrics is rooted in the call rising in congregational leaders for an outward, missional way of life. Clarifying your call is about more than the people who identify as members.

Reggie McNeal observes that in most churches today, the indicators of success or effectiveness are skewed inward toward the attractional, programmatic, and institutional factors of Christendom rather than outward toward participation in God's mission. (*Missional Renaissance: Changing the Scorecard for the Church*)

The journey of centering includes a willingness to rethink the scorecard. Of course, there is value in knowing how many people come and how much money is received but, as we have discussed, these are lag metrics that can be applied to any organization. The church's metrics need to grow out of scripture, history, and tradition. Take a close look at the First-Century church through Paul's autobiographical letters to see that Christians have always wrestled with living out their faith. Early in the history of the church, there is tension between Peter (kosher for all) and Paul (kosher for none) that created divisions.

Take a moment to reflect on Paul's words as he talks about what it means to live "in Christ."

> Finally, beloved, whatever is true, whatever is honorable, whatever is just, whatever is pure, whatever is pleasing, whatever is commendable, if there is any excellence and if there is anything worthy of praise, think about these things. Keep on doing the things that you have learned and received and heard and seen in me, and the God of peace will be with you. I have learned to be content with whatever I have. I know what it is to have little, and I know what it is to have plenty. In any and all circumstances I have learned the secret of being well-fed and of going hungry, of having plenty and of being in need. I can do all things through him (Christ) who strengthens me. Philippians 4:8-9, 11-13

Identity emerges over time and discovering it is more of an art than a science. Rather than a final "Purpose statement," this step in the process focuses on drafting a congregational purpose that will be revisited.

As the purpose is articulated, it should affirm the very existence of the congregation and reflect its theological perspective. The church can never exist solely to serve the needs of the people gathered. There is a bigger vision, or purpose, because it is part of God's purpose.

Typically, the purpose of the congregation rises to the surface once the values have been articulated. When done well, this takes the outward focus to a whole new level, not just emphasizing the importance of serving or understanding needs of others, but explicitly saying, "This is who God has called us to be as a people."

Purpose describes the unique contribution your congregation makes to its world—the neighborhood. For this reason, a congregation's purpose will not be the same as any other congregation's. Purposes are not interchangeable. They speak out of the soul of the ministry, shining a light on what God is doing in and through this particular faith community.

Take LEAD, for example. LEAD's purpose has not changed over time although most everything else has evolved in response to what we have learned from those we serve, our stakeholders.

LEAD exists to grow leaders with a deep, bold, consequential faith. Our core values are:
– Empowering Christian Leaders
– Transforming Faith Communities
– Influencing the World

Our purpose drives everything we do. It informs our goals and metrics. As an entrepreneurial organization, we revisit these words constantly, tweak them occasionally, and change the way we live them out over time. Some on the LEAD team are great at standardizing what we do so that we can strive for excellence and create space for new experiments. Others have to be reminded

that we can't follow every shiny new idea that comes along. The tension created by this push toward standardization and the pull toward new pilots creates a innovative environment for the team and, more importantly, a great value for stakeholders.

As leaders work to articulate a motivating purpose, congregations can examine their history and current reality. It is crucial for a purpose statement to cut straight to the heart of what the congregation is about and to bridge the past, present, and future. It should use words that make sense to someone outside of the organization while at the same time singing the heart song of those in the congregation.

When done well, the congregation's purpose will sound "right" to the congregation. There should be a relief in the system that comes with a feeling of centeredness. Words chosen after carefully listening to the congregation make the purpose statement ring true and inspire the hearts of those who will carry out the goals within those values.

Narrowing the purpose for impact

Annually, the leadership of the congregation can narrow the overall purpose to create a one-year focus. For example, if the congregation's purpose is to be a "Sacred space for busy people to worship, learn, and connect with a generous God," the focus for one year might be on generosity. This does not mean other ministry stops, but it does mean that generosity drives the theme for that year's goals.

3. ACT: Values and Purpose

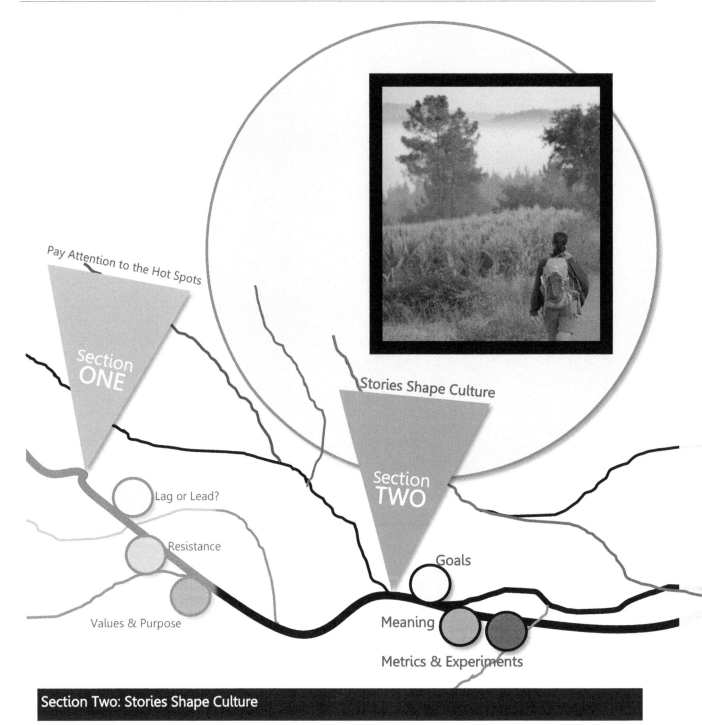

Pay Attention to the Hot Spots

Section ONE

Stories Shape Culture

Section TWO

Lag or Lead?

Resistance

Goals

Values & Purpose

Meaning

Metrics & Experiments

Section Two: Stories Shape Culture

Chapter 4. Goals—How does recognizing adaptive vs. technical challenges directly impact success?

Learn to set goals and identify purpose

Chapter 5. Meaning—How can metrics be used to deepen and expand the congregation's story?

Reflect on maximizing God moments

Chapter 6. Metrics and Experiments—How can leaders identify and test metrics?

Act on strategic pilots together

Section Two: Stories Shape Culture

¡BUEN CAMINO!
(bwane kah-MEEN-oh)

This is the ritual greeting shared among pilgrims on the Camino, friends and strangers alike. Buen Camino literally means "good journey" or "good path" or even "right track," and it represents more of a blessing than a polite head nod.

It is interesting how a shared language can shape the culture. There is something calming, welcoming, and connecting about looking into the eyes of total strangers to offer and receive a blessing. And this blessing is shared over and over, all day long, while walking the Camino de Santiago. Shopkeepers, farmers, people driving by, and fellow pilgrims from across the world find connection in these simple words.

This greeting contains an implied "we are here if you need anything" support system. It is hard to describe, but it provides an energy that pulls you forward when you are tired and lets you support others when they are worn out. We were not naïve enough to think everyone was to be fully trusted, yet we were open to the possibility of trusting. This vibe could be felt from early in the morning as pilgrims started their day, some before the sun even rose, into the late afternoons when, hot, dirty, and tired, we were ready to enjoy one of the famous Spanish tortillas (a delicious potato and egg torte very unlike anything in Central America) with a glass of wonderful Spanish wine.

It turns out that walking the Camino is a cultural experience with a shared language and more. Pilgrims on the Camino share a communal story, a way of being that is understood by total strangers on their way to the same destination. We were all wrapped up in the same story with the undeniable awareness of our own vulnerability and the realization of our interdependence. Oddly enough, we were church together.

Think about this:
The word church in the Bible comes from the Greek word ecclesia, which means a called-out company or assembly. Wherever it is used in the Bible, it refers to people, not buildings.

Consider these three definitions of church:

1. The body of Christ, a local assembly or group of believers most often meeting in homes. (1 Corinthians 1:2; 2 Corinthians 1:1; Galatians 1:1-2)
2. The body of individual living believers, the people themselves. (1 Corinthians 15:9; Galatians 1:13).
3. The universal group of all people with a shared story who trust in Christ through the ages, past and future. (Matthew 16:18)

What made us church on the Camino was the Holy Spirit moving through our lives, practices, and stories. There are countless versions of what it means to be God's people on the move together. These two key points connect directly to the metrics work:

⊕ An awareness of God moving in your life, wherever you are, can open up your view of church.
⊕ Shared stories shape culture and reveal God's story among God's people.

Once removed from the framework of traditional worship space, church can be everywhere. Opening up the definition of sacred space encourages a God-view that sees the Holy Spirit on the loose. Thinking about church in new ways gives leaders ideas about metrics that can transform their own faith imaginations.

Collecting data is always easier than interpreting what the data is telling you. The goal is to move from the collection of data on a few key metrics to information that has meaning. For the data to have integrity, the meaning must be found within the stories that the numbers reflect because it is the stories that make meaning in a relational community, not the numbers.

Your brain and storytelling

Verne Harnish, in his book *Scaling Up: How a Few Companies Make It...and Why the Rest Don't,* writes this:

> Two things have been crucial to humans' survival. One is pattern recognition, the most important cognitive skill connected to extreme success in any field. The other is hearing. You can hear prey long before you can see, touch or taste it (or it tastes you!). Hearing stories, information, and even numbers connects more deeply to our pattern-recognition capabilities than staring at an Excel spreadsheet.

On the flip side, brain-wave scans show that we need to talk out our problems. When we speak, the prefrontal cortex of our brain – the source of executive and cognitive power – lights up like a Christmas tree. (p. 178)

Many business people have discovered the power of storytelling in a practical sense; they have observed how compelling a well-constructed narrative can be. But recent scientific work is putting a much finer point on just how stories change attitudes, beliefs, and behaviors.

A decade ago, labs discovered that a neurochemical called oxytocin provides a key it's-safe-to-approach-others signal in the brain. Oxytocin is produced when people are trusted or shown a kindness and it motivates cooperation with others by enhancing a sense of empathy, an ability to experience others' emotions. Empathy is important because it allows people to understand how others, including those with whom they work, are likely to react to a situation.

Well-crafted stories motivate people to act by engaging the brain, increasing oxytocin and thereby increasing trust between people. It is easy to look at numbers and feel dejected or numb. It is not as easy to ignore or reject a compelling story that puts into words what the numbers are saying.

When leaders are able to share both facts and stories, they have hit the jackpot, engaging both the analytical and emotional sides of the brain at a meaningful level.

Stories are not only better at interpreting data, they are better at eliciting the desired responses from the data.

Harnish concludes his book with this statement:

> Success belongs to those who have these two attributes:
> ⊕ An insatiable desire to learn
> ⊕ An unquenchable bias for action
> (p. 237)

Both are motivated by information shared in stories. Think about the parables. Jesus knew that stories make meaning.

Stories make metrics transformational

Collecting data is not the destination. The value of identifying lead metrics is realized when the measures are used for individual and congregational transformation.

The point is to use the data to get clarity on stories of transformation. Whether people are aware of it or not, the stories people tell themselves, and those that are yet to be named, shape who they are. These stories can be intentionally named and claimed, told and retold to shape the narrative of the community. This ancient tradition is both formative and transformative.

Once you and your congregation identify stories, ask:
⊕ Is this the story we mean to be sharing?

⊕ Is this the story of our faith?

⊕ Is our story big enough and inclusive enough to welcome others?

⊕ Is God the subject of our stories or is God just showing up in them, added as an afterthought or not mentioned at all?

People are sharing stories in everything they do. Just as leaders may be surprised by the way people outside of their congregation talk about their church (or don't talk about their church), they may be shocked to hear the narrative they are communicating without realizing it.

Insider eyes are keeping leaders blind to the stories they tell. For better or worse, metrics can reveal these stories as a starting place for a rebranding effort.

Stories shape culture—two stories

Think about the civil rights movement and the ritual story relived each year at Holy Week.

⊕ Both are stories of faithful people expressing their understanding of God's love for all people.

⊕ Both are still shaping culture.

The civil rights movement continues today in response to the misuse of power and issues of respect and human rights in areas from race and sexual orientation to immigration and gender equality. The Black Lives Matter movement is an example of a timely reclaiming of civil rights work for today.

The #metoo movement that started with Tarana Burke in 2006 in order to spread awareness and understanding about sexual assault in underprivileged communities of color is another. By connecting survivors with survivors, this movement has freed women from the stigma of sexual harassment in real time.

These stories are driving culture in public arenas and intersecting with faith communities to varying degrees. They provide ways to engage in meaningful movements that make a difference in your faith as they move the faith story from the Bible and the church to the street.

The Passion of Christ, or Holy Week narrative, has a smaller circle of influence—or does it? When "Ashes to Go" captures the imagination of the unchurched and countless people show up on Facebook wearing ashes, there are people who are swept into the Holy Week drama through a side door.

These disconnected examples give leaders a glimpse of how old yet essential life-giving stories can use new delivery systems to shape culture. Leaders in the church can learn a lot by noticing how other movements have started, made an impact, and moved through a natural life cycle from peak to what may feel like decline. As significant as the civil rights movement was in shaping our world, it did not complete the work of equality for all. There is no end to the ways in which people oppress one another across the globe. This movement is alive and impactful today as a historic marker, yet it is also alive today in many new versions as people are using new language and new platforms to tell the story and lead change.

The church can continue to hold on to its most-valued historic gifts while, at the same time, being reformed and re-visioned with new language and new platforms as it has ever since the first story was told.

God is faithful to a future story even when leaders are not feeling hopeful. People of faith have thrown up their hands in despair about the state of the church today. These same cries of frustration can be heard echoed in the Psalms and the words of the prophets with similar refrains. We can go forward with full confidence.

To connect these ideas to faithful metrics, what stories are bubbling up that need to be told, or retold in new ways, to shape and reshape the culture?

What you measure will influence that story as it reinforces values, purpose, and goals— intentionally or accidentally. Leaders have the opportunity to shape the future with the metrics they set today.

Is your congregation telling a story that aligns with your values, purpose, and outward, adaptive goals? If not, how can you set metrics that will shape your stories of forgiveness and grace for new ears?

Please Note: Chapters 4-6 in Section Two invite leaders to set clear goals, create moments worth measuring, and experiment with stories. Leaders who choose to skip Section One and start here instead are missing the opportunity to validate shared values and clear purpose. As time-consuming as this may seem, LEAD encourages you to affirm Section One before moving into Section Two.

Metrics with clear goals and purpose inspire ministry

4. Goals

Setting metrics before identifying clear goals is like walking the Camino without embracing the ¡BUEN CAMINO! vibe. It can be done, but it misses the opportunity for transformation.

When done well, a few strategic goals give shared values new meaning and movement within and beyond the congregation. Goals create the narrative that drives momentum, guiding the story that leaders will celebrate and broadcast.

Each year many congregational staffs and councils set goals with the hope that new things will happen. For some, setting the goals is an exercise that drives behavior; for others, the goal setting is more of a ritual than a true commitment to action. Then there are leaders who admit that their congregation rarely sets goals. And yet, ministry happens. Or does it? Who is doing it right?

LEAD's consultation work has shown that congregations that identify values and set a short list of goals have a better chance of being aware of God moving in their midst. This is especially true if the goals align with the congregation's values and are reinforced with intentional metrics. The congregation's capacity to experience the always-present Holy Spirit increases when the congregation

nurtures a culture that is on the lookout for God's stories to shape life.

By creating a short list of strategic goals, leaders can break through the inertia of "what we did last year." The comfort and simplicity of repeating ministry patterns year after year provide a low-anxiety goal-setting system without leaders even realizing it. This can be a trap resulting in more programming than people can bear and it is more dangerous than it sounds. Simply moving the dates of events forward from year to year without intentional conversation, puts more than goals at risk. Over time, leaders begin to shift from God-focused to get-it-done focused, missing the value of Christian community. The congregation's entire reason for existing is inadvertently driven by the calendar with unspoken lag metrics built in. As the number of people engaged in each program decreases, the real casualty is the congregation's confidence that the Holy Spirit is alive in their midst.

Not all goals are created equal.

At the risk of offending leaders, the worst goals LEAD has seen:

⊕ Focus on people who have left the church. These people have already voted. They can still be your friends but they cannot drive the ministry of the congregation. The grief is real but getting stalled here is toxic.

⊕ Focus on a core group of members of the congregation without including the neighbors, people who use the building, or children, youth, and families in the goal-setting process. Ignoring these people creates an inward movement and will lead to stagnation and ultimately to decline.

⊕ Focus on finances without paying attention to worship, discipleship, faith formation, learning, and spiritual practices. It is these practices that set congregations apart from other nonprofit organizations. Ask, "What makes the church different?"

⊕ Lack focus because the goal is too large, overwhelming, or does not have a plan. A goal to "grow the church" is not helpful as it fits all these categories. BHAGs (big hairy audacious goals) can be great if they come with a plan. Incremental steps forward that emphasize small wins work best.

⊕ Lack inspiration because the goal is too small, administrative, or targets too few to create commitment. A vision to clear the closet clutter or organize the archives may seem reasonable but doesn't feel like Jesus inviting Peter to get out of the boat to walk on the water.

Technical vs. adaptive

Great congregational goals pay attention to the challenges surrounding the congregation's opportunities to live deeply into shared values. These challenges may be adaptive or technical or some hybrid of the two. These working definitions from Heifetz, Grashow, and Linsky are helpful:

Technical challenges are those where the problem is *clear*, the solution is *clear* and there is *clarity* on who owns the work. In other words, these are challenges we know how to solve and our current systems support the problem-solving process.

Adaptive challenges are those where the problem requires *learning*, the solution requires *learning* and the work is relegated to the *stakeholders*.

The technical and adaptive challenges are where the problem is *clear,* the solution requires *learning* and the work belongs to those in *authority* as well as to the *stakeholders*.

This way of thinking about goals may be new to congregational leaders, who are inclined to set technical goals and avoid adaptive goals, sometimes unintentionally, for two reasons:

⊕ The lines of authority are established, with an inertia to self-preserve their power in the system.

⊕ The solution is known, comfortable, and often feels more trustworthy.

Essentially, when leaders know what to do and who should do it, they are ready to lead forward. Everything makes more sense and feels more familiar to their usual way of life.

Solving technical problems works because the solutions are known and fit easily into their current way of being church together.

Technical goals, like increasing nickels and noses in worship, feed the practice of setting lag metrics. Ushers know how to count people. Tellers know how to count money. Leaders are aligning their technical skills to set goals and to measure their success. This behavior feels normal because it's been done forever and it reinforces current thinking.

Shifting to adaptive goals that are usually measured by a series of lead metrics requires new learning. It is less intuitive.

Think about learning a new operating system on your cell phone. The device is the same but the newly installed system is hard to get used to, yet it can be done.

Shifting to adaptive goals means rethinking the problem being solved and makes leaders feel vulnerable because there is so much to be learned. Again, like the new cell phone operating system, it can be learned but it will feel clumsy at first.

Facing personal truth about learning curves

One big area for growth is directly related to your own leadership. As part of the congregation's system, leaders are part of the challenge. Chances are good that the people in the church are some of your closest friends or even members of your family. Part of your personal resistance to change can be related to concern about helping people you care about understand what and why change is needed. Managing your resistance to learning is the first step to leading others through new thinking. In the end, it is because of the trusted relationships that new thinking can be adopted.

This is where the cell phone metaphor breaks down. People adapt to cell phones without a relationship. A faith community's operating platform is trusted relationships.

Technical Goals (established authority and known practices) ➡ Reinforce current thinking, preserve way of life

Adaptive Goals (new voices and experiments) ➡ Reinforce new learning, create future possibilities

Feeling vulnerable is uncomfortable. The irony is that by moving into this vulnerable space in your relationships, they can mature and deepen. Strengthening healthy relationships is a good leadership investment. However, using relationships to manipulate a situation or gain power will result in power struggles and brokenness. One way forward is to focus on a few goals in strategic areas. Setting adaptive goals within one or two congregational practices is enough to create some movement in most congregational systems. When one part of the system shifts, the rest of the congregation will feel the impact like ripples in a pond. There is an opportunity to use goals as leverage for future ministry change by carefully considering the ministry of the whole congregation before deciding on which practices to influence and focusing on one or two strategic goals.

What are your congregational practices?

Congregational life is typically framed by practices that grow out of scripture and tradition:
⊕ **Worship**
⊕ **Partnership** (with neighbor)
⊕ **Spirituality**
⊕ **Community**
⊕ **Care** (for each other)
⊕ **Generosity**
⊕ **Leadership**

Each of these practices is an expression of the faith. LEAD draws on research that affirms these practices, although the names themselves may be different. These practices can be found operating at some level in all congregations regardless of size, geography, or culture.

In this time of unprecedented change in the world, it's important to address these practices in strategic ways. Practices are an outward expression of core values. These values can be seen in how time and resources are spent. You practice what matters to you. You can also recognize practices you need to grow into as faith deepens.

Do a quick reality check on your own congregation to test this idea.

⊕ What are the standing committees, teams, task forces, or whatever you call them that people do not want to sign up for?
⊕ Where is it the hardest to recruit leadership?

Chances are good that the answers to these questions shine the light on the congregational practices that are least aligned with the values of the people in the congregation. People don't want to invest their time or resources in practices they are uncomfortable with. Like it or not, the current population gathered does not have a commitment to the practices that are always without leadership. This may be Christian Ed, the Church Council, or any other part of the congregation's ministry.

In LEAD's experience, the practice that struggles the most is evangelism. Even if people sign up for it (or are talked into it), there is typically little output from the Evangelism Team. There is anxiety around evangelism that reveals a lot about values, skills, and the deeper theological framework. Yet evangelism is at the core of the Christian movement.

A deep look at evangelism is outside the scope of this field guide. What is relevant to this discussion, however, is the pushback that reveals a clash between what the congregation says is a practice and what the congregation really practices.

Identifying faithful metrics that fit inside of your values, purpose, and goals begs the question: If your congregation resists evangelism (or any other practice), is there another way to express this practice so that it resonates with the values of the people — or at least creates space for them to grow into it?

Congregational practices may be driven by the past—"we have always done it that way before"—or they may be constitutionally driven. Most congregational constitutions outline ministry that accomplish functions but do not prescribe the exact form these functions must take. In other words, there is room to be creative within the constitution.

This drives the question: Do you really need to keep doing congregational practices that are outside of your values?

Is it possible to be the church if you don't do evangelism? Teach the faith? Have governance in place? Care for each other? Respond to human need and suffering all around us?

Can you as leaders tasked with setting faithful metrics establish new patterns of congregational practices that fit within your values?

What would Jesus do?

It is hard to imagine throwing any of these practices out—but it is exciting to consider new ways of expressing them that can reenergize the system.

If the current leadership does not engage in this life-giving conversation, how can it truly embrace an adaptive approach to ministry? By virtue of being leaders, they are called to mess with existing congregational relationships to scripture, theology, tradition, the congregation, and those not in the church.

The most compelling reason for leaders to boldly risk rethinking congregational practices is the current results, or lack thereof.

LEAD is offering new language and definitions for a larger vision of each of the typical practices, with one exception. We have left evangelism off the list.

The e-word has not worked for the church as it is currently defined. We want to boldly rethink this by suggesting that everything on the list include evangelism. Sharing faith is not the work of only a few people on a committee.

Evangelism is defined as the intent to expose the love of God, through Jesus Christ, to the world.

LEAD sees this as an important component of everything Christians do. Evangelism is not one value or a practice on a list, it is the waters all Christians swim in by virtue of their baptism.

The sacrament of Holy Baptism in the *Evangelical Lutheran Worship* states this responsibility clearly:

> ...to live with them among God's faithful people, bring them to the word of God and the holy supper, teach them the Lord's Prayer, the Creed, and the Ten Commandments, place in their hands the holy scriptures, and nurture them in faith and prayer, so that your children may learn to trust God, proclaim Christ through word and deed, care for others and the world God made, and work for justice and peace. (p. 228)

With this in mind, try out the seven practices within the context of the values, purpose, goals, and ultimately metrics for your congregation. (A chart with definitions is on page 73.)

The seven Congregational Practices include:
⊕ **Worship**
⊕ **Partnership** (with neighbor)
⊕ **Spirituality**
⊕ **Community**
⊕ **Care** (for each other)
⊕ **Generosity**
⊕ **Leadership**

Each of these practices offers opportunities for setting goals. As you read the descriptions, consider which are most critical to God's mission for your congregation at this time. Remember that the fewer goals you set, the more likely you are to achieve them. Once goals are set, you will move on to choosing one or two lag metrics and a few lead metrics for each goal.

Start thinking about setting goals before reading about each of the seven practices. Imagine that your congregation has a dashboard with a few significant goals that are aligned within your shared value system. Imagine there are lag and lead metrics under each goal. Imagine that leaders, both staff and council, are attentive to these lead metrics weekly and monthly as the goal comes to life. Here is a list of questions to consider:
⊕ What is the focus for this year's goals? What would make the biggest difference if the leadership invested here?
⊕ Who would be best at leading this effort?
⊕ Are there clear metrics that leaders can record to show progress toward the goal?
⊕ How can the goal(s) be widely owned by the congregation?

⊕ Where will the stories be told that will increase momentum?

As a couple of goals come into focus, the next step is to wonder if the goals are inwardly or outwardly focused.

Congregational practices tend to focus inward in response to the opportunities and needs of the people gathered and outward in response to the opportunities and needs of the people who are not part of the congregation's worshiping community.

The most effective goals will pay attention to both the need to focus inward and the need to focus outward. Making the gathered community the priority misses the huge reality that no one actually lives at church. (Not even the staff.) If leaders intend to shift the trajectory of the congregation's ministry, attention to what happens in the rest of their lives is essential. As more than 30 years of research attests, faith is formed more in the home than at church.

In his book, *The Scattering: Imagining a Church that Connects Faith and Life*, Dwight Dubois points out that the gathered worshiping community is also scattered as it leaves worship for daily life. He writes:

> Congregations need to learn how to talk about scattered ministries openly and concretely. Members are already talking concretely about their lives in private conversations and small groups. When we gather in fellowship, we talk about our work, families, volunteer activities, and recreational pursuits. The problem is that we are not trained to talk about these activities as the means by which God is at work through us for the welfare of our neighbors. (p. 125)

Theoretically, this kind of thinking blurs the lines between inward and outward goals. However, attention to the outward reality of faith life is counterintuitive to leaders who focus solely on their church.

Attending to outward goals is a paradigm shift that makes space for valuing more than what happens when people gather. Outward-facing goals have a higher chance of resulting in transformational metrics.

Space can be created in the gathered community for people to share stories of their ministry in daily life.

Opening up a value system that includes caring for elderly parents and small children is essential to the church of the future. Goals and metrics can be written that celebrate all the ways people serve one another: through nonprofit boards, by volunteering in community projects, as people living out their vocation, and more. Outward-facing goals shift the stories that will be told. The energy that had been spent on survival can become energy for ministry in the fullest sense of the word.

The congregational practices

Each of the seven Congregational Practices are introduced here. As you read through them, embrace the tension between inward and outward movement. For more in-depth descriptions, including sample goals and metrics, go to waytolead.org/metrics. LEAD also offers a digital dashboard and consulting in each of these Congregational Practices to support goal setting and the metrics associated with them.

Worship

How do faithful worshipers experience God in your congregation's worship? Answering this for yourself is a great place to start.

How do first-time worshipers experience God in your congregation's worship? If you are not sure, either ask them or try worshiping someplace else to get the "first-time" feeling yourself. The idea is to become aware of the inward and outward possibilities for goals related to worshiping God, which is the central purpose of the church. For more information on setting goals and metrics for Worship, go to waytolead.org/metrics.

Partnership (with neighbor)

Typical congregational language like outreach, service, or mission misses the real opportunity for deepening faith in ourselves and others. Language matters because it shapes behavior. The image of partnership is very different than the image of outreach; partnership grows out of relationships that have shared interests. For many congregations, service is project-focused with a one-and-done mentality that doesn't include building ongoing relationships. While these have meaning for participants and some added value for those served, imagine what could happen if local, domestic, and international partnerships were created with people working side by side to reduce human need and suffering? This is more aligned with the intent of the baptismal covenant listed on page 62. For more information on setting goals and metrics as we Partner (with neighbor), go to waytolead.org/metrics.

Spirituality

In many places, Sunday school has run its course as a viable approach for teaching the faith. Congregations have an opportunity to experiment with new ways of growing Biblical literacy, wrestling with faith questions, and practicing faith at home, work, school, etc.

The shift from youth ministry to family ministry in the 1990s was a relief to leaders who realized the impossibility of shaping a life of faith in a few hours a month. But just naming parents, caregivers, grandparents, and other adults as primary for faith formation has not produced the hoped-for results. The preference for age-level, siloed Christian education is somehow attached to what it means to be a good church—a hidden metric.

Setting new goals and metrics that create conversations around the ministry of the home is helpful only if the story is told widely and accompanied by a cry for adult discipleship. Most parents feel inadequate when it comes to their own faith, much less the faith formation of their children. There are wonderful resources available and creative approaches to be tried. Goals and metrics are needed to change the mindsets of the adults who personally benefited from youth ministry models of the past. For more information on setting goals and metrics as Spirituality, go to waytolead.org/metrics.

Community

The early church, described in Acts 2:26-47 and throughout Paul's letters, grew as people spent much time together in the temple, broke bread together in their homes, and cared for the needs of the people. To be blunt, this is in tension with today's institutionalized church that gathers for worship, meetings, and programs. What is missing is the genuine community that is irresistible to people seeking meaningful relationships.

Living in community is not just about fellowship after worship. People living in community show up for each other in hard times, celebrate in good times, and hold each other in high regard with healthy accountability. Genuine community self-regulates by pointing out when people are out of bounds and reaching out to people who may not even realize they need it. All of this happens because the people really know each other.

When leaders use the word "community," what comes to mind is their congregation. Yet sadly, too few people experience deep community in church. For more information on setting goals and metrics for Community, go to waytolead.org/metrics.

Care (for each other)

This Congregational Practice is related to Community and some congregations may even combine the two. Often referred to as pastoral care, Care (for each other) is focused on meeting people's deep relational and spiritual needs.

It is time to move beyond the expectation of the pastor doing all the care. While there is a role for the pastor, the pastor is the spiritual leader of the congregation, not the professional counselor, caregiver, or home visitor.

This practice is vital to adult discipleship. Equipping the congregation to care for one another beyond the membership is one way people will mature in their faith. Imagine people equipped to accompany those who are grieving a chronic or terminal diagnosis, preparing for marriage, becoming parents, struggling in the midst of a divorce, or transitioning to a new stage of life, or even death. Decentralizing pastoral care is about multiplying caregiving, not just freeing up the pastor's time. For more information on setting goals and metrics for Care (for each other), go waytolead.org/metrics.

Generosity

In the book, *The Paradox of Generosity: Giving We Receive, Grasping We Lose*, Christian Smith and Hilary Davidson share their research-based finding that giving makes people happier. They state that the happiness derived from acts of organ donation, volunteering, and charity fundraising can all be explained by the sociological and psychological perspectives of how adults understand and demonstrate generosity.

This is a great place to start when thinking about metrics that might inspire giving. Imagine increasing happiness all year long through strategic efforts to celebrate, appreciate, and encourage giving. This sounds much more inspiring than a stewardship campaign.

Experts in this field of generosity know that every congregation can increase its giving with particular strategies. LEAD believes that if congregations simply learned a few new practices from their nonprofit partners, giving would increase. Yet many are uncomfortable talking about money. For more information on setting goals and metrics for Generosity, go to waytolead.org/metrics.

Leadership

The decision-making, strategic-thinking, organization-development roles of congregational leaders are changing. Clarity of roles, systems with built-in accountabilities, and helpful new digital resources offer more efficient ways of leading congregational life. In most cases, there is more freedom for creativity than leaders realize, even within their existing constitution.

Leadership can be learned. Congregational leaders that make spiritual leadership of the community a priority are heading in the right direction. Out of a deepening faith and a growing trust, these people have a better chance of creating a revitalization movement in their congregation than an outside consultant. Alignment between the staff and council or board is essential as ministry and governance work together to discern vision and to set and accomplish goals. For more information on setting goals and metrics for Leadership, go to waytolead.org/metrics.

Yellow Flag: Do your technical or adaptive goals face inward or face outward?

Going a little deeper into goal setting, leaders can set both technical and adaptive goals for inward and outward purposes. The implications of this are significant. Leaders will be disappointed if all their goals are inward *and* they hope for missional growth. In order to have missional growth, goals must have an outward posture. It is possible to set outward technical or adaptive goals.

Remember, technical simply means that leadership will draw on existing expertise while adaptive means going off the map for new learning.

Goal	Technical	Adaptive
Inward Facing the congregation ———→	Inward Technical Using your current systems and expertise to do a better job inside the congregation.	Inward Adaptive Experimenting with new ways of making decisions, practicing faith, and being the church inside the congregation.
Outward Facing the neighborhood ———→	Outward Technical Using your current systems and expertise to do a better job in the neighborhood or world.	Outward Adaptive Experimenting with new ways of making decisions, practicing faith, and being the church in the neighborhood or world.

Inward goals are what LEAD refers to as back of the house goals. These goals are about making an organization or congregation function better. There is always an opportunity to improve here. The real danger comes when all the leadership energy is spent looking inward with an expectation of outward results. They rarely find what they are looking for.

For appreciable gain, leaders need to risk outward goals. These are goals that engage the neighborhood, the country, or the world. The chart below is helpful in defining inward and outward technical and adaptive goals.

Let's revisit one of the worst goals listed and brainstorm technical and adaptive goals to help illustrate these concepts.

Imagine you have set a Worship goal to engage more people in God's mission.

Example of an inward technical goal

An inward technical goal could be to recruit people who have left the church over the past few years to come back. This is frequently the default because it is perceived as a quick, easy fix. While this may *feel* like the easiest path forward, in the end it is the most risky for the future of the congregation. Encouraging friends who have left the church to return seems like a natural step because you may still be in relationship with them. You know what to say to them and you can usually guess how they will respond. You may even be hoping that if they return, the future will look more like the past.

Example of an inward adaptive goal

An inward adaptive goal could be to deepen the congregation's capacity to truly welcome new people. After carefully considering the many ways this might happen, let's imagine that the leadership chose to create a sister with a nearby congregation different than themselves.

Let's imagine that this congregation is a different ethnicity, speaks a different language, or is not Christian. The inward adaptive goal might be to have quarterly dinners with this sister congregation. This is inward focused because the people involved are those already in both congregations.

Imagine telling stories of these dinners. The first meal might include only the staff, council, and key leaders from both communities. The second could grow to include a larger group of people. By the end of the year, this sister relationship or dinner club might have tripled in size.

Are you starting to think about goals and metrics here? Are you also hearing the potential internal Judger-Learner conversations taking place? Can you feel people growing deeper in their faith, asking harder faith questions as they grow in their relationship with others?

Example of an outward technical goal

An outward technical goal could be to partner with neighboring organizations (not just churches) in responding to the urgent needs of people in the world. This might be hosting a homeless ministry in the building once a week, starting a food pantry, or offering summer day camp.

These are all ways a congregation can expand its relationship with the world beyond itself, if the stories of what is happening get told both when people gather and in their homes. These are all technical because you know how to do them, or, if you don't know, you can easily find experts to help you execute these goals. There is expertise for hosting homeless groups, food pantries, and summer day camp. All these engage the community in life-changing ways, and in most cases they expand relationships and fit within congregational values.

Example of an outward adaptive goal

An outward adaptive goal might be to listen to the parents of the children in the _____ (you fill in the blank: preschool, Scout groups, school across the street, or food pantry client base)_____ to build new relationships and discover their God questions.

This listening (LEAD calls this The Tune In Process) requires listening to people in the congregation *and in the neighborhood*. This means approaching people you do not know as the experts. It means opening up your own Learner and putting Judger on pause so you can hear God's voice through a stranger.

This might look like:
1. Listen to 10 parents who bring their children to __X___, in the next three months.
2. Create one experiment that responds to the listening for a quick win that deepens relationships.
3. Share the insights from the experiment with the congregation and beyond in one year. (Tell stories, use photos, etc.,)

Can you see how this opens the way for adaptive experimenting? An outward adaptive goal results in discovering new stories, learning the God-questions others have that may surprise you, and wrestling with your own new God-questions.

Success from this kind of outward-facing adaptive goal could be a collaborative team of people with those who use the food bank or go to the school and those who lead worship working together to create a meaningful experience for worshiping God in ways outside the traditions of your usual worship.

What changes in this adaptive process? The stakeholders!

The power to determine the shape of worship becomes a shared power, an adaptive challenge that invites new learning.

Why adaptive goals produce greater results

As we discussed, the spectrum of goal setting moves in this way:
⊕ Inward technical
⊕ Outward technical
⊕ Inward adaptive
⊕ Outward adaptive

All goals can fall in one of these categories. Yet not all goals will produce effective results. For the biggest impact, leaders need to risk setting outward adaptive goals.

Remember, adaptive goals are filled with unknowns and an eagerness to learn. They are likely to yield less-than-hoped-for results, on occasion, yet in a time of great change, they are the only goals that can produce the kinds of breakthroughs that people of faith should expect from each other. They create the space that allows for new learning in ways that technical goals rarely do.

To review: Choosing the path of what may, at first, feel like least resistance, can be the start of a downward spiral. By trying to talk the people who left the church into returning, leaders unintentionally create obstacles for new learning and growth.

Numerical growth and growth in discipleship, both fine goals, are healthier when they engage new people in adaptive work. The neighborhood is filled with new potential that is essential to the future of the faith community's viability.

Leaning into your faith is (and always has been) the key to setting God-size goals. Small steps in an outward direction are the way goals can drive mission.

Goal setting framework

There are many proven processes that can offer a technical *and* adaptive way forward. This is a hybrid where the problem is *clear,* the solution requires *learning,* and the work belongs to those in *authority* as well as to the *stakeholder*s.

LEAD recommends using an appreciative inquiry model for goal setting that affirms what God is already doing in the congregation. Once goals are in place, setting metrics and gaining ground with faithful metrics becomes easier.

The SOAR process (Strengths, Opportunities, Aspirations, and Results) also has proven effective for setting strategic goals.

Unlike the commonly used SWOT analysis (Strengths, Weaknesses, Opportunities, and Threats), SOAR is asset-based and engages all levels and functional areas of the congregation.

There is the possibility of inviting new voices into the process to open up imagination and expand mindsets; some congregations include neighborhood leadership in their SOAR process.

The focus is on the strengths of the congregation (and, if they are represented in the room, the strengths of the neighborhood and partners) rather than perceived threats and/or weaknesses. The SOAR process is more closely aligned with the work of adaptive leadership because it makes space for mapping new territory. More information about the SOAR process is available at waytolead.org/metrics.

New to setting goals? If your congregation has not set goals in the past, now is the time to start. Clarifying goals is critical to setting faithful metrics.

Quarterly goals

Ultimately goals will be broken down into quarterly increments so that they drive

leadership behavior. Amazing ministry happens when there is alignment between the annual goals of the congregation, the quarterly goals of the staff and council, and the monthly goals of each accountable leader (paid or unpaid).

By breaking goals into quarterly bite-size pieces, leadership is building in places to celebrate, opportunities to share stories about new insights, and time to make course corrections, if needed.

If this kind of goal setting is new, consider using LEAD's Annual Roadmap, a goal-setting resource designed for two-day leadership retreats.

Write your goals in pencil. Revising goals throughout the year to incorporate new perspectives is fine. However, if your goals are constantly changing, they will be meaningless. It takes practice to get a rhythm for goal setting. The most important thing is to stick with it even when the going gets rough.

Congregations, like individuals, are always wrestling with managing their resources of time and money. Tension around setting priorities is inevitable, but as the focus on goals becomes a regular leadership practice, the congregation will benefit from this investment.

Note: Some leaders have a preference for long-range planning. In general, this was more helpful in the past than it is today. Living in a time of rapid change has made it virtually impossible to predict beyond three years with any success.

If you have doubts about this, think back to the use of telephone booths only 15 years ago. Imagine a group of people making a strategic plan to maximize the use of phone booths after noticing fewer and fewer people using these spaces to talk on the phone. All the while this conversation is going on, another group of people is designing the device you have in your hand right now. If you were to measure the success of the telephone by the use of phone booths, you would be seriously depressed.

You may be struggling to imagine what new forms of church God will reveal in the future, but you will never be able to see them if all you focus on is goals related to the past. There isn't time to create long-term goals because they will be obsolete in only a few years—if not sooner.

Fast-growing congregations with more than 300 people in weekly worship will want to have strategic plans that span three to five years at most. For most smaller congregations, annual goals are more effective. In either case, a short set of annual goals are needed to create momentum.

Remember, the goals you set will be used to drive metrics and the metrics' results will inform next year's goals.

Yellow flag

LEAD wants to raise a yellow flag if your congregation's goals include building a new,

larger structure. We recommend building only if it is absolutely necessary. In many communities, using the existing structure(s) is better stewardship of resources, less of a drain on leadership, and more likely to engage innovation. Think about the neighborhood. Build only when there is a clear vision for using the building for mission beyond the people who are paying for it.

Renovations, on the other hand, may be urgent and important. Investing in maintenance, updates, and renewal of space offers endless opportunities to rethink the building's use in alignment with the congregation's purpose and values. Looking outside those who are currently gathering is the key. Imagine who might be using the space in the future by listening to the needs of the neighbors, learning what resources are already available, and brainstorming what ministry opportunities might be on the horizon for the congregation. LEAD's 10-step process, Tune In, helps congregations listen for God's call to mission in the neighborhood and world.

Share the goals

Goal setting is usually most effective when done in partnership with the staff and council. These leaders are entrusted with the visionary responsibilities on behalf of the congregation. Inviting the neighbors to share in the process provides new perspectives and a wider view. Once set, goals must be shared with the congregation in a variety of ways to strengthen their impact, hold leaders accountable, and build broad support.

Goals can be shared in meetings, sermon series, conversations, or adult forums; at congregational meals; on T-shirts, bulletin boards or banners; or through websites, social media posts, newsletters (paper or digital), conversations, etc. By using a variety of delivery systems, more people are exposed to the goal story. Even more importantly, wide communication lets the community celebrate goals together while creating momentum for forward movement.

Chapter 5 introduces the idea of creating meaningful moments that impact the culture of the congregation. This is the practice of turning goals into stories. These stories can create momentum as they take on a life of their own through repeated telling. The church is part of a long line of storytellers who have had the outward, ever-adapting goal of passing on faith from person to person.

Congregational Practice	AKA	Inward growth metrics	Outward growth metrics
Worship	Worship or church	⊕ Celebrates sacraments ⊕ Reflects theology ⊕ Deepens spirituality ⊕ Builds relationships ⊕ Involves generations ⊕ Expands culture ⊕ Moves the heart	⊕ Expects new people ⊕ Excels in preaching and music ⊕ Sees God in all things ⊕ Practices forgiveness ⊕ Engages senses ⊕ Welcomes with intention
Partnership (with neighbors)	Outreach, service, or mission	⊕ Widens worldview ⊕ Expresses faith in daily life ⊕ Responds to human need ⊕ Names injustice and systems of oppression	⊕ Builds new or deeper relationships ⊕ Reduces suffering ⊕ Changes systems of oppression
Spirituality	Christian ed, parish ed, faith formation, learning	⊕ Learns and teaches the faith ⊕ Increases Biblical literacy ⊕ Expands theological lens ⊕ Encourages questions	⊕ Encourages new learners of all ages ⊕ Increases God-awareness ⊕ Shares rituals for home and life
Community	Fellowship	⊕ Celebrates and grieves together ⊕ Practices grace and forgiveness ⊕ Celebrates diversity	⊕ Shares meals ⊕ Reflects on God's presence in life's challenges and joys ⊕ Welcomes with intention
Care (for each other)	Pastoral care	⊕ Listens deeply ⊕ Shows up for each other ⊕ Sees strength in weakness ⊕ Creates systems for responding to needs	⊕ Listens and builds relationships ⊕ Cares for strangers ⊕ Pays attention to the needs of all ages
Generosity	Stewardship	⊕ Builds generational awareness ⊕ Nurtures giving all year ⊕ Extends invitation often ⊕ Thanks constantly	⊕ Values generosity ⊕ Celebrates giving time, resources and gifts every day
Leadership	Administration, staff, council, governance	⊕ Establishes clear roles and accountability ⊕ Offers room to grow and vision ⊕ Expects commitment to learning and leading	⊕ Provides accessible systems for decision-making ⊕ Uses Learner mindset ⊕ Listens with great curiosity and models this for others

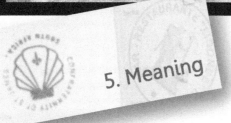

5. Meaning

Sacred stories are cultivated

There is always more to a good story than the obvious. The countryside of Galicia, Spain, (and beyond) is filled with these interesting little structures, many with small crosses. They were all built with a similar long, narrow, rectangular footprint and a peaked roof, each rising above the ground on flat slabs of stone. Made of brick, stone, or sticks, they were a curiosity, and we tried to imagine their purpose as we walked.

It turns out, the truth is much more practical than our imaginations! These charming structures were grain storage units in the 15th century.

Better known as "hórreos" (in Spanish the "h" is silent), they were once used to store food and the flat stones called "muela" that form the base of the structures were perfectly designed to keep rats or other animals out of the harvest. Small doors and a staircase provided access to the inside.

Without this background information, these little beauties were magical and mysterious. With the history, they told a story of the people who lived and worked the land we were walking on. Knowledge created meaning in a way that just looking at the architecture could not. Seeing the connection between those ancient people and our Camino gave the journey deeper significance. It provided a "value added" component to an already sacred experience.

Your buildings have stories too—stories that hold the past while at the same time giving meaning to the future. Reimagining the use of your buildings is part of the gift the church can offer the local community. When buildings are hoarded or enshrined as historical landmarks, they miss the purpose for which they were first built—as places to worship God and partner with the neighborhood.

What if you used your values, purpose, and goals to cultivate the story you tell about your church buildings?

How can the story be expanded beyond fundraising, construction, and use of the space?

There are powerful moments when congregations recognize that their resources, including the buildings, were given as gifts and can be re-gifted. Leaders are discovering that their sacred spaces are more holy when shared and are leveling up, increasing your congregation's impact by freeing up the use of their buildings.

Moments like this are God moments that open congregations and their people up to opportunities bigger than themselves.

Over time, meaning may be unintentionally assigned, like the space in many churches known as the "cry room." A label like this implies that noise from children is

problematic in worship. When congregations have a shared value of families deepening faith and set goals to welcome new families, renaming this space in a more positive way helps point the way. What are the images and stories created just by changing the name "cry room" to one of these?

⊕   Family Room
⊕   Comfort Room
⊕   VIP Room
⊕   Play Room
⊕   Joyful Noise Room

This is only one small example of aligning buildings with values, goals, and purpose. You can write your own story.

Opening the doors

Church buildings are being opened to share space with fair trade stores, farmers' markets, community gardens, health clinics, food banks, yoga studios, English as a second language classes, and nonprofits that serve the neighborhood youth and elders. This is good news. Stories of some of these congregations can be found at waytolead.org/metrics. More on buildings as a goal can be found at waytolead.org/metrics.

When leaders begin to develop goals that are informed by the congregation's clear purpose and shared values, they have new stories to tell. They can create metrics that expand the story to include a faith with a much bigger understanding of what it means to be God's people. Shared values can be a path forward.

Gestures of welcome that are essentially self-serving are not expressions of hospitality. Just like children know whose homes they are welcome to be their true selves in, the neighbors know when the church really cares about them. Going through the motions by setting up a welcome station, adding smiling ushers, and other only skin-deep efforts miss the point. More on deep hospitality can be found at waytolead.org/metrics.

What does this have to do with metrics?

Jesus insisted his disciples feed people even when they weren't in the mood; then they counted the leftovers. The lag metric could have been how many were fed, but Jesus was making a bigger point about abundance. So in this story, the lag metric is actually how much was left and the lead metrics might be how many people were willing to share, how much actual food was shared, or what happened that encouraged people to share. As a reminder, a lead metric is something that can be influenced. Generosity is taught, molded and inspired by others.

What story do you want to tell?

God is calling you to be the church that opens the doors wide, gives freely to all, and still ends up with leftovers to share. This is your heritage. This is truly leveling up. You are part of a people that never has everything they need in order to do what God is calling them into, yet they continue to respond. You are the church that sincerely leans into your faith.

This is very different from the church that feels they don't have enough so they don't even start. The movement from scarcity to abundance is clearly an act of faith. It has to do with putting your values into action, even if they are risky. Values that do not influence behavior aren't really values. Saying you are people of faith and then only acting out of your own known resources is not being truthful.

So, what can get you from point A (scarcity mentality) to point B (faithful risk-taking)? The answer is a messy intersection of your values, trust that the Holy Spirit is moving, and living with conviction in the story God wants you to tell. This is what gives meaning to metrics.

LEAD defines meaning as something with significant influence and heartfelt value that is aligned with a larger purpose.

Even successful congregations that value service can begin to atrophy when they separate themselves from their own stories.

Service as part of a checklist for faithfulness is not a valued metric. This kind of community outreach or social service with a handful of passionate, committed people serving on behalf of the congregation is not enough. People who have been transformed by service will always serve—they just have to. It is part of who they know God has made them to be. It is *who they are*. This is transformational—for them. However, this does not transform the whole congregation they represent.

Even when it's done well, why isn't servanthood transformational for more than the servant?

It's not that those who are deeply committed to the relationships they have locally or globally don't want others to join them, but they don't have the bandwidth to carry this burden along with all they are already doing. They are not letting the church down; the system of the church had been designed to protect the church from transformation. Leaders with a passionate heart for mission often fail to infect the larger community because the church sees these as a program or a project or something "they do." This is in contrast with a ministry fully owned by the congregation.

How does this go viral? How does the depth of discipleship in the hearts of these leaders infect others in the community?

LEAD has struggled with this for years. We see passionate, loving, transformed people eager to share their stories with their congregations and who want the congregation to feel the love and join the party. Remember the song, *It only takes a spark to get a fire going*. So where is the blaze?

The system of the church is working against discipleship. In fact, the system is a giant distraction.

Come with us up to the balcony for a brief reflection exercise.

A Few Observations from the Balcony

A handful of people (or a youth group) travel to Peru or a Native American reservation or an Immigration Center along the U.S.-Mexico border on what they expect will be a mission trip, even though the "getting ready" meeting taught them about the ministry of accompaniment.[6]

To their surprise, they spend the week listening to the stories of the people, learning about the culture, and joining local people in worship. It is more of a "being" than a "doing" experience. As they tear up during the final reflection, with hearts filled with a new view of God and God's people, they realize they have few words to describe this journey.

Then the panic sets in and they begin asking: How will we share this transformational experience next Sunday, in just an hour (or whatever time is allotted for telling the story)? Where do we start? We haven't had time to really absorb all we have experienced ourselves. Now we have to talk to the congregation. They still think we came to "help the poor" but really, we were the ones who were changed.

Learn more: [6]ELCA Ministry of Accompaniment http://download.elca.org/ELCA%20Resource%20Repository/ACCOMPANMENT_BIBLE_STUDY_INTRODUCTION_PAGES.pdf?

These faithful souls know their congregation so they dumb down the transformational experience and play up the pictures of the cute children. They share a few short what-the-trip-meant-to-me stories before they have had time to find language to articulate how the liminal experience measured a true 10 on their personal Richter Scale. If they dare tell about an issue of injustice they observed, someone in the congregation will likely respond with a question or comment that shakes the confidence of the speaker and minimizes the meaning of the experience for the speaker.

The audience can see the emotions, hear the stories, and appreciate the impact this had on their lives. But nothing has changed the deficit in the budget, the decreasing number of people in worship, and the fact that no one wants to serve on committees.

Next year, a few more people go on the trip and some of the faithful from the first trip find a way to go again because they are falling in love with God and can't resist.

Eventually the funding for this kind of mission dries up and only a few people can afford to go without endless fundraisers that become a secondary mission themselves.

Think about this:
⊕ How can these stories move from the edge of the congregation to the center? From the few to the many?
⊕ How does the fire really spread?
⊕ Who are the people that can help leverage this experience for greater influence?

⊕ What are the systems that could be put in place to help people with a deepening faith grow even deeper?

Meaning is made by the stories that are heard the loudest and the most often by those with the power to change the system. One goal of this field guide is to introduce leaders to the opportunity to level up by finding meaning in stories that are all around them. Travel is not required.

Stories will be told. The questions to be asked are: What are the stories? Do they point to God or are they part of a negative, downward spiral that points to the pain and brokenness in relationships?

The role of the leader is to shape the story by equipping people to be storytellers. Growing a community of people on the lookout for God moving in and among them is a value to be taken seriously.

Once you can clearly state that something has meaning, you can begin to see how it may become a lead metric. Leaders can collect stories of transformed people that are central to the evidence that shared values influence outcomes. Some congregations do this automatically, but most need to be taught how to see their named values being expressed in meaningful ways outside of their usual frame.

Values, purpose, and goals that influence metrics and spark shared stories have the power to change a lag-only congregational culture.

A great example of the power of storytelling comes from a leader of a church in a small town. He learned the value of listening at a LEAD seminar, and took this to heart personally. He even contracted with a professional coach to help him learn to listen.

As the value of listening took root in his life, he began to realize how much he had missed by not listening deeply to his own family and to his clients. He became aware of all the great stories he had missed out on over the years because he had not really listened to people. In fact, he realized that instead of hearing the stories people were sharing, he was listening to his own thoughts as people talked with him.

As a leader on the council, he realized he was increasingly impatient with church leaders who weren't listening to God and to each other. He became aware of people missing out on each others' stories. Out of this frustration, he launched a monthly listening space where the congregation could gather for the purpose of listening to each other share their stories. Over time, this congregation has moved from being inwardly focused to being outwardly focused by listening to God, to each other, and to their neighbors.

These stories, shared in community, about being present for each other are significant. They are informing the congregation's metrics. When leaders in this congregation imagine lead metrics, they recognize that the amount of time they spend listening is a measure that influences the lag metric of more adults in weekly worship. The more they listen, the more people notice God moving in their lives and the deeper faith grows, calling them to weekly worship.

Thinking strategically

Creating God moments, like this, out of a shared value and desired future story does not happen accidentally. Getting from point A to point B is messy and at the same time strategic. Faithful leadership actually plans to tell stories of God's activity with confidence that God is up to something in their lives. As we have discussed, there is a remarkable lack of confidence in church leaders today. This lack of confidence reduces pride and certainly waters down any courage they might muster to lead change. It makes leaders apprehensive about responding with a God moment, yet these are exactly the moments to live for as people of faith.

The best part is that leaders don't have to make up stories about God. They are all around. Waking up to what is already happening, naming it for what it is, and telling the story—this is what metrics with meaning are about.

In *The Power of Moments: Why Certain Experiences Have Extraordinary Impact*, Chip and Dan Heath teach how to mark these moments. They offer story after story of successful moment makers. People tend to remember flagship moments, what the Heath brothers call the peaks, the pits, and the transitions.

These are the defining moments of life. While the whole book is helpful for implementing faithful metrics, the section on pride is especially compelling.

What the Heath brothers are not writing about is the way God is present in all of these moments.

The Heaths are clear:

> You can't manufacture "moments of courage." but you can practice courage so that when the moment demands it, you will be ready. (p. 182-183)

They go on to say successful practice of courage comes with training and graduated practice of what feel like dangerous tasks that are likely to be encountered. They cite work done in exposure therapy where people are gradually introduced to fears, one step at a time. In their words, "managing fear–the goal of exposure therapy–is a critical part of courage."

From leader to leader

If congregational storytelling can be this powerful, imagine what would happen when leaders in congregations started telling their stories to each other. Imagine how God's movement would be amplified—and how people would be moved.

Congregations can work together, learning from each other. Old anxieties about being in competition with each other are more of a bad joke than ever in this fast-changing world.

Working in learning cohorts with other congregations provides an opportunity for leaders from different congregations to hold a mirror up to each other, reflecting meaning in stories that might otherwise be missed. The deep aha moments that help you know what to measure are as likely to come from the outside as from someone who is part of the system. It is hard to have clarity on your own story while you are living within its narrative.

LEAD has found that healthy leaders engage peers in conversations that deepen faith. They seek out people who will challenge them, hold them accountable, and offer new insight. They are curious learners that feel empowered in relationships, not threatened. The trusted conversations that are generated by leaders are ripe with stories that invite transparency. They encourage support as others point to where God is moving in your life, offering new meaning to what might otherwise be dismissed as mundane.

Leadership networks, small peer groups, and prayer partners are the most nimble leadership communities when it comes to leading change. Leaders aligned around shared values, goals, and purpose can start a movement. The best model for this can be seen in the life of the apostles.

As you ponder the metrics, values, goals, and purpose of your congregation, how could the church building be leveled up to expand the meaning of this space? What story does this space tell the neighborhood about faith?

For example: One congregation has turned their unused classrooms into studio space for local artists.

What congregational ministries are ripe for new meaning? What are new stories that could be told that shift the lag metric associated with them?

For example: One congregation realized their children's choir was down to three children yet the neighborhood was filled with this age group. They started a neighborhood children's choir that sang in both Spanish and English. Worship, caroling during the holidays, and music in the park were all on their agenda. Songs were sung in both English and Spanish. This Community Children's Choir gave new meaning to neighborhood outreach and the young voices who gathered together on Sunday mornings became friends.

Who are the peers in your life that help you make meaning of the mundane? Or who are the people you want to invite into peer group?

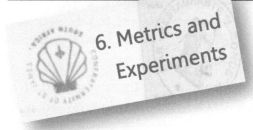

6. Metrics and Experiments

Measuring what matters most

Up to this point, everything in this field guide has been designed to clear the path for meaningful, faithful metrics. As you begin articulating metrics, the following is assumed:

⊕ Leaders have an understanding of lag and lead metrics.

⊕ The congregation has shared values.

⊕ Most people are clear about the congregation's purpose.

⊕ Leaders and/or the congregation have a short list of adaptive or technical goals for the year.

⊕ Leaders and/or the congregation understand that numbers have limits, but leaders can make meaning and moments from the stories that are told.

The question to consider now is:
Which Congregational Practice(s) will be targeted for lag metrics in the next year?

It's best to begin with one or two lag metrics and their associated lead metrics. Choose the lag metric that aligns with your annual goals, fits within your values, and supports your overall purpose. Over time, lag and lead metrics can be set for every congregational practice.

From here on out, values, purpose, and goals will be understood as the frame for faithful metrics.

The power of framing metrics

There are three gifts in using the values, purpose, and goals as a frame for congregational leadership:
⊕   Creativity loves constraint.
⊕   Control loves constraint.
⊕   Calibration loves constraint.

Creativity loves constraint.

The art of transforming limitations into advantages is a valuable leadership skill when it comes to framing metrics. Most people see constraints as restrictive and adversely limiting, yet outward, adaptive leadership goals can turn scarcity into abundance over time. Many great leaders have steered their organization into, not away from, a constraint using the constraint as an opportunity to experiment.

Consider crisis situations, for example. No matter how prepared people may think they are, there are always moments when a crisis catches them off guard. A crisis is a constraint because the old ways of doing things are no longer possible, as when the church building floods, the budget is not met, or staff resign unexpectedly. People tell

heartwarming stories of being there for each other and working together to solve problems and meet needs, sometimes even life-threatening ones. These stories are filled with people who surprise themselves and others with new behaviors, a willingness to risk, or unexpected generosity.

Creativity loves constraint, even constraint that comes during hard times.

Congregation after congregation can tell stories of times in their history when, faced with a challenge, they created something new. People do remarkable things, from the simple idea of congregations hosting neighborhood Halloween parties, started in the 1980s after the Tylenol scare[7], to the meaningful ways congregations open their doors to refugees, immigrants, and homeless in their communities. They rise to the occasion when the going gets...constrained.

This is a perfect time in history to respond to the pressures of a changing world by moving toward new opportunities. The congregation's frame is exactly what is needed to put limits on the current situation and inspire new visions for ministry.

Constraint can also be expressed through a real or perceived sense of urgency. Many leaders resist making decisions until the risk of not changing is greater than the risk of

Learn more: [7]Johnson and Johnson responded to Tylenol products being tampered with by engaging the media as part of their crisis communication strategy. This led to an increased concern for malicious tampering of Halloween candy. Community centers, congregations, and schools responded with alternatives to trick or treating. https://www.ou.edu/deptcomm/dodjcc/groups/02C2/Johnson%20&%20Johnson.htm

change. LEAD encourages a proactive use of constraint before financial, spiritual, and emotional resources are diminished. Why wait for desperate times to step up and lead the church into the future?

Constraints on things that matter most, such as the congregational practice of Spirituality, can liberate the church from old practices like Sunday School and invite a search for new ways to teach the faith. Constraints on finances can spark imagination around ways of sharing or inspire generosity. Leaders don't have to wait until ministry hits bottom to try something new. Constraints can be built into goals and metrics, serving as tripwires in advance of crisis.

Without any constraint, it is too easy for leaders to get stuck in thought patterns from the past. Leaning into its frame encourages the congregation to participate in using metrics to shift outcomes. People support what they help create; alignment is gold as the metrics are named and used to drive results.

Control loves constraint.

The frame shapes the playing field so that those who have responsibility for oversight and control can lead with confidence. They can be assured that boundaries are in place to protect what is most valued. In a similar way, those who want freedom know their limitations building confidence that the risks they take are within reason. Metrics provide focus inside the frame.

The frame offers an opportunity for change in alignment as well. Big decisions like staffing or new ministries can be tested against the frame. New questions can be asked about old ministries as they relate to the frame. A program or ministry of the congregation can be celebrated if it fits in the frame, tweaked to fit if only a few changes are needed, or deleted if it clearly doesn't fit.

These hard decisions become easier when the frame is used as a guide. The frame frees leaders from making decisions based solely on relationships as the objective nature of the previously agreed on frame is engaged. Working with congregations, LEAD has used the frame to help them stop doing ministries that were outside the frame and to focus on strengthening ministries within the frame.

Calibration loves constraint.

Finally, the frame can be used to drive metrics themselves. This is key as leaders will not measure everything—only the metrics that are in alignment with the frame.

Brainstorming metrics for each goal benefits from constraints. There is an art to effective brainstorming within the frame. LEAD's tips on brainstorming are at waytolead.org/metrics. Keep in mind that your first ideas will most likely not be your best ideas, so an investment in brainstorming will result in a bigger pay off.

By beginning with lag metrics tied to goals, there is an unspoken agreement that these goals are significant among the leaders of the congregation. As we have mentioned, leaders understand that metrics will not be set for every one of the congregational practices in the first year. It is possible that over time each practice will have lag and lead metrics associated with it, but that is not a reasonable starting place.

Part of calibration is defining the starting place. You won't know if the lead metric is moving the lag metric unless you have a baseline set. It is essential to ask, what is the status or baseline of the metric right now?

This may require some truth-telling or at least more transparency than usual. Data is seldom the topic of congregational conversations, so articulating a starting place may feel awkward at first. There is no way to move forward with metrics unless there is a willingness to name things for what they are. This can be done without blame or shame as facts are shared. Time spent pointing fingers is a distraction from identifying metrics and can be an ongoing distraction when interpreting meaning later.

Calibration may also include defining the lag metric in greater detail. Clarity reduces confusion and shapes expectations. Leaders should resist the urge to use generic language when writing metrics. The more specific the metric, the better.

For example, imagine the lag metric is to: Increase neighborhood partnerships by 50% in the next year, these are some things you will need to know up front:

- How many partnerships exist right now?
- How do you define "neighborhood partnerships?"

Using this example, think about this:
- How are you currently measuring partnerships? Is it:
  - Relationships with the people who receive services from the congregation's food pantry?
  - Relationships with the people who work at the food pantry who then have a partnership with the clients that benefit from the food pantry?
  - Relationships with the people who donate the food or money to purchase food for the food pantry?
  - All three?

Each of the examples above would require different metrics that result in different data and tell different stories.

A 50% increase in relationships with the people receiving food would look very different than a 50% increase in relationships with the people who are working at the food pantry or a 50% increase in relationships with the people donating to the food pantry.

What is the intent of the lag metric?

Without clarifying the lag metric, it would be impossible to identify helpful lead metrics. Once lag metrics are drafted (not finalized), it is time to brainstorm lead metrics for each lag metric. The lead metrics should be just as easy to quantify so that reporting is simple and objective.

Using the same example, imagine the different outcomes that could be generated depending on the lag and lead metrics. Here are a few to make the point:

If the lag metric is to increase the partnership with people who receive services from the food pantry by 50% in the next year, then a few lead metrics could be:

⊕ Develop a trusted relationship with the people who work at the food pantry by listening to them, learning from them, and even working with them.

⊕ Develop a trusted relationship with the people who donate the food, or money to purchase food, to understand why they give, to share stories of clients, and to share new goals.

You can see that by getting specific, some metrics that initially felt like lag metrics can actually become lead metrics.

Just to refresh your memory:
⊕ **Lag metrics have already happened by the time you get the data.**
⊕ **Lead metrics are the indicators that leaders strategically set, and that have the potential to change the lag metric.**

Carefully evaluate the list you brainstormed using the definitions above. Are they specific, measurable, attainable, realistic, and timely[8] enough?

If you are unsure which metrics will be the most helpful for a certain goal, use this reflection to shape the conversation. Imagine that you are stranded on an island. You have no contact with your faith community except for three indicators that will tell you everything you know about your beloved church back home. You are praying that goals are being accomplished and everything is staying on track until you can return.

Ask yourself:
⊕ What do you need to know in order to have confidence that congregational goals are staying on course?
⊕ What three indicators are indispensable?
⊕ If you could receive a weekly or monthly report or story, what would you need to hear?

Your answers to these questions can focus the development of lead metrics. Be aware that brainstorming lead metrics usually results in more lag metrics! Use the definitions to affirm that you are selecting lead metrics from the best possible list.

Once there is a lag metric with two or three lead metrics for each goal, it is time to test the process. These metrics will remain in draft form for at least three months.

LEAD recommends that the full list of lead metrics you initially brainstormed be kept for a few months. After a little time testing the lead metrics, it can be helpful to revisit the list to determine if the lead metrics you chose were the best ones.

Learn more: [8]SMART Goals—https://www.mindtools.com/pages/article/smart-goals.htm

When identifying metrics, it is normal to edit, refine, and tweak them or to start over during the first few months. Once the metrics are in place, the leadership can focus on running experiments to change the lead metrics and ultimately shift the lag metric.

Missional experiments

As you know, faithful metrics are intended to measure what matters. Generally, leaders will work toward the metrics they set and the metrics will produce *something*.

As we mentioned earlier in this field guide, congregations have typically focused on the lag metrics of bodies and bucks, which results in decreased confidence and increased congregational reluctance to set adaptive goals. *That is something*.

LEAD hopes that by first clarifying values, purpose, and goals, the *something* is more outward and adaptive. In other words, you are trying to create metrics that join in God's mission with a focus beyond yourself.

Once leadership is ready to try out the lag and lead metrics, it is time to experiment. The adaptive process invites leaders to place small bets on shifting the metrics. Testing lead metrics over time is the only way to discover whether the best indicators have been identified.

Experimenting by field testing lead metrics is both exciting and anxiety producing. Some leaders' hearts will stop beating when they

consider anything that has the potential to fail; yet an experiment is exactly that—a chance to test out a new idea. Other leaders will feel energized as they receive permission to be creative.

There are times when persevering is exactly what is needed. Some lead metrics will take time before the lag metric shifts. It is a good idea to commit to a window of at least six to nine months before making a decision to pivot or persevere. There is more about this practice in the conclusion.

Lead metrics that involve new learning are likely to require time to germinate. Increasing generosity as a spiritual practice, for example, may take longer to bear fruit if the congregation is not already accustomed to giving regularly. That does not mean the lag metric should be abandoned, but it may mean the lead metrics need to be tweaked over time to find the most effective way to teach generosity to a particular population.

Keep in mind that when we talk about experiments in this field guide, we are not talking about random acts of program ministry. The intentional work of clarifying values, setting adaptive goals, identifying purpose, and considering congregational practices all make experiments more likely to succeed because they offer something more strategic.

Congregations that run program after program hoping to find the one that will save the day are wearing themselves out. Using LEAD language, these people and congregations are Out of Breath, both physically and spiritually. (See *Sacred Valley*[9] for more on this.) In fact, LEAD research shows that people already know that programs won't save a dying church or revitalize tired leaders, much less inspire new people with the grace of God.

Here is a snapshot of what a strategic experiment tied to metrics might look like. Notice that there is an intentional leveling up in the intentional outward focus, in this set of lead metrics. Each level of experimentation has the potential to nudge the lag metric in a different way as the value grows in the community.

Goal:
Equip adults to talk about their faith in daily life.

Baseline:
When surveyed, 20% of adults in this congregation indicated that they felt comfortable talking about their faith in daily life.

Lag metric:
Triple the number of adults with a faith language in six months.

Lead metric with meaning:
25 adults using cell phone videos to tell their story faith stories on Facebook in the next six months.

Courageous experiments:
Level one: Training Camp where adults learn to make cellphone videos and post them on Facebook.

Level two: Training camp where adults identify their Spiritual Type and are introduced to a variety of faith practices.

Level three: Commitment from 10% of the adults in the congregation to talk about their experience with faith practices to each other in worship or in a small group.

Level four: Commitment from 5% of the adults in the congregation to record themselves talking about their faith practices and answering the question, why do faith practices matter to me?

This is just one example. There could be dozens of great experiments that impact the lead metrics, move the lag metric, and ultimately achieve the goal. And there are many other lag metrics that could be considered for this goal. This example did not include just one experiment but rather a series of experiments that incrementally moved toward the lead metric.

Some strategic points worth noting:
1. The goal was clear.
2. There was a baseline survey indicating a starting place.
3. The lag metric is specific and measurable.

Learn more: [9]Peggy Hahn shares more about the different types of leaders and the implications for growth in *The Sacred Valley.*

4. The lead metric is specific and measurable and includes a story component.

5. Level One training engages adults in something they are already motivated to learn and may have already conquered. Some people who join the experiment will not need Level One.

6. Level Two introduces people to something they want or are curious about and makes it personal. Everyone is welcome. This training camp may be offered in several different ways, including face to face or digital with website support. (waytolead.org/metrics to assess Spiritual Types and to dig into faith practices.)

7. Level Three: Only a small percentage of people constitute a win.

8. Level Four: Even fewer people are needed to launch an experiment that might ultimately become a movement. The videos may be shared on Facebook or in worship, with everyone who participated, at any level, being celebrated.

9. The door is opened for more to participate. Everyone wins as the congregation recognizes that faith practices work for ordinary people, including their own friends and family.

10. Next steps are endless and, again, should be strategic.

Courageous experiments push people along the path you hope they will go, creating a movement along the way. They require low investment on the front end, yet new learning will take place and new questions will be asked. For more on deepening adult faith with lead metrics, go to waytolead.org/metrics.

But really, what if we fail?

Experiments are all about learning how to select the best lead metric(s) to shift the lag metric. Most will not be home runs on the first try. The beautiful thing about experiments is the learning that emerges and the confidence that is built over time.

Leaders running experiments are invested and energized. Yes, they can get disillusioned when they fail if people are blamed, or if people are not thanked and celebrated for trying, or if people are alone on the journey. Yet there is an opportunity for leaders who are willing to experiment to be protected when they function within the frame. In this way, the congregation can birth new ideas as church councils bless and back those willing to experiment.

Brainstorm experiments you might use to shift the metrics you identified earlier. Remember, this is only an exercise, so dream big.

Take a chance—engage others in your design process. Who can you bounce your ideas off of in a way that is life-giving? This is not about reaching out to your "rubber stamp" friends. It's about exploring with feet-on-the-ground great-thinking types.

In their book, *The Practice of Adaptive Leadership: Tools and Tactics for Changing Your Organization and the World*, Heifetz,

Grashow, and Linsky make it clear that the role of a leader is to manage the heat. If there is too much complacency, it is time to turn up the heat. If the anxiety in the system gets too high, it is time to turn down the heat. Leadership means taking strategic risks. Running experiments is a great way to disrupt the system without cranking the heat up too high.

Use the outline on the next two pages to gather your work. Gathering decisions on one piece of paper is key to sharing this process. A print-ready worksheet is available at waytolead.org/metrics.

Use this worksheet to pencil in your notes. A one-page goal sheet makes communication easier.

Purpose of the Congregation:

Our Shared Values:

Adaptive (Outward) and Technical (Inward) Goals for the Next Year:

Goals	Strengths	Opportunities	Aspirations	Results or Lag Metric	Leadership

Metrics:

Lag Metric
Lead Metric (Outward)
Lead Metric (Inward)
Lead Metric (?)

Lag Metric
Lead Metric (Outward)
Lead Metric (Inward)
Lead Metric (?)

Lag Metric
Lead Metric (Outward)
Lead Metric (Inward)
Lead Metric (?)

Quarterly Experiments:

Jan.–March	July–Sept.
April–June	Oct.–Dec.

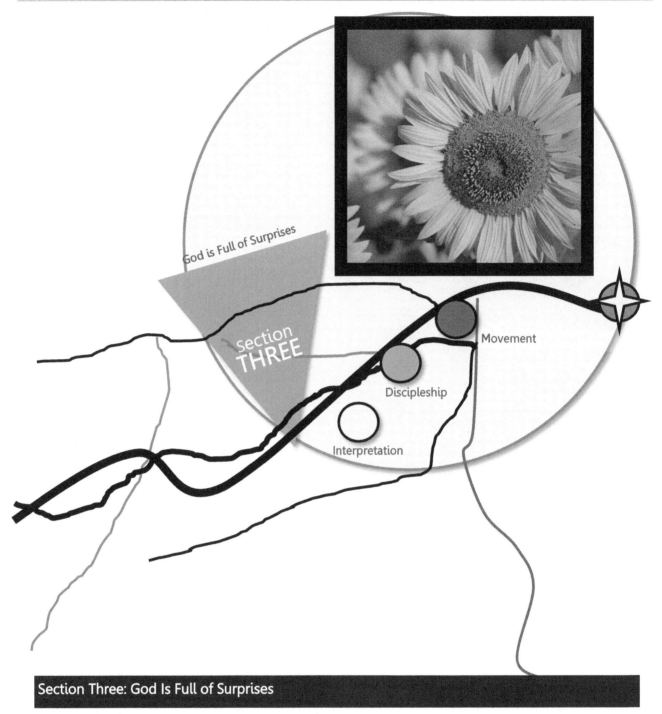

Section Three: God Is Full of Surprises

Chapter 7. Interpretation—How do leaders know what the metrics are saying?
   Learn how to understand metrics

Chapter 8. Discipleship—Can leaders measure discipleship and still be faithful?
   Reflect on metrics for discipleship

Chapter 9. Movement—How can faithful metrics expand relationships?
   Act out of relational intersections

Section Three: God Is Full of Surprises

Expect to be amazed

One morning, we set out earlier than usual to avoid the heat. Starting before the sun is up gives you a different perspective. We walked mostly in silence except for a tune in our head accompanied by these words:

Listen in the silence, listen in the noise, listen for the sound of the Spirit's voice.[10]

On this day, our path began through a tunnel of trees that formed a dark arch over our heads as the sun slowly rose.

We were lost in our own prayers, observing the day coming alive around us as time went by.

Then, as we walked around a particularly dark corner, we got our first indication that something was about to change.

Everyone who turned this corner let out an audible gasp. The experience was literally breathtaking: Acres and acres of fully open, extremely bright sunflowers shining in the morning sun. The contrast from what the morning had been was shocking. We were like little children playing in the flowers. It was exhilarating. It was a God moment with a story to share!

[10] *Listen in the Silence* by singer/songwriter Linnea Good—http://www.linneagood.com/

It may sound like overreaching to say you should expect surprises as you interpret data that comes from your metrics; yet, why not?

The Holy Spirit is alive and working in your congregations and in you.

This is what it means to be people of faith. The fact that you expect God to *do something*, to act in your life, *is* exhilarating.

It is also freeing to realize that you don't bear full responsibility for the future of the church.

You can live with confidence that there will be a church. Looking back even as far as scripture, you can feel secure in the many ways church has shown up over the centuries.

While you may grieve the changes in the church, you know God is up to something in the midst of the whirlwind.

Your part is to try to catch up, at least a little bit. Transformational metrics are one way forward. In moving to identifying the metrics you will test in your own setting, be open to surprises. By measuring in new ways, you may discover new paths forward. This can be encouraging but also a little intimidating.

It helps to remember that the lead metrics claimed for a period of time are a starting place. If the metrics aren't working, change them. Consider them an experiment rather than a trap.

From outward to inward

In this section, the work shifts to discovering what your metrics are telling you. It is not enough to *have* metrics. They are simply one set of indicators to guide leaders in decision-making, planning, and visioning. The preparation and act of setting metrics is an outward movement that drives leaders to think beyond themselves and the congregation to joining in God's mission. This outward movement is essential as you raise your awareness of God moving in every part of life.

Making meaning out of the metrics is an important feedback loop for the congregation. Up to this point, the focus has been to look outward. Interpretation is an inward journey as leaders use what they have learned to go to work in the congregation.

Your own curiosity about the meaning of the metrics set may be the best part of the whole process. As you evaluate the information gathered, you may be surprised and excited by new stories and insights. At the same time, you may also recognize that there could be better metrics. This iterative process creates great leadership conversations.

Creating faithful metrics is only as valuable as their capacity to serve the purpose of the church.

This is a good place in the journey to check your own biases and assumptions. Review the discussion on shifting from a Judger mindset to a Learner mindset in Chapter 2.

Everyone has lenses they use to make sense out of the world. This is one way the brain keeps you from getting hurt. Leaders have a responsibility to expand their lenses as they get to know diverse perspectives. This capacity is essential to adult learning and to effective leadership. Your personal self-awareness and growth is important as you lead using faithful metrics. In the end, transformation and revitalization of congregations come from people growing a deep, bold, consequential faith.

Use the space below to note a few of your blind spots.

⊕ Where have you been surprised in the experiments and metrics?

⊕ Do you tend to switch from Learner to Judger? Or the opposite?

⊕ What is God revealing to you?

7. Interpretation

Appreciate the markers

When walking the Camino de Santiago, the pilgrim's credential, or passport, is a meaningful part of the journey. Each unique stamp collected along the way represents an experience.

Some stamps are readily available in bars (what we would call coffee shops) for a small donation, others require walking out of your way to see an ancient ruin or visit a chapel. They are like little gold stars for weary pilgrims, yet they are much more. They mark memories of conversations with other pilgrims, of aha moments, of blistered toes ... They tell the story of the journey.

The mile markers on the path are helpful encouragers as they let pilgrims know how far they have to travel to reach Santiago, but they are less relational. The yellow arrows and little shells pointing the way are specially important when walking through towns with traffic and crowded sidewalks. They build confidence that you are on the right path. Recognizing that pilgrims from across the world have walked this same path for thousands of years is deeply spiritual; being part of this sacred journey is part of why we walk.

Yet nothing really tells the story like the passport stamps. They remind us of what matters most in the story—the relationships we are nurturing with God and each other.

As you begin to interpret metrics, you hold something sacred in your hands. We are part of a long line of leaders, from Abraham and Sarah forward, who have wondered what God is saying to them. Prayerful, thoughtful interpretation is in tension with the "get it done" culture. Leaders have a responsibility to look at what is being said, or not said, with a grateful heart filled with God's grace.

This helps leaders remember that not all metrics, lag or lead, are created equal.

Learning from metrics on the first round

Learning from metrics is a messy process. Testing metrics, running experiments, and reflecting on what we learn is an ongoing process. Lag and lead metrics can be tweaked as the timeline unfolds. That is the beautiful part of an experiment. There are creative moments where new questions and new understanding can help us create nuanced language that makes big differences. Don't be afraid to tweak the metrics in real time.

Setting transformative metrics identifies measures that are most likely to shift the lag metrics that reflect the congregation's frame. Over time, it becomes clear whether the best metrics were put in place. If you missed the mark, try again.

LEAD thinks of this as starting with the best possible MVP (minimum viable product) and then upgrading along the way. In other words, don't wait until everything is working perfectly to begin interpreting data and testing metrics.

Adaptive leadership requires the courage to try before every piece of the experiment is finalized. In this spirit, leaders give themselves freedom to make changes as they learn from their "draft" metrics, and the metrics themselves become part of the experiment.

What happens to the data once you have it? Applying meaning to data is a delicate thing. Again, leaders have to check their personal biases when they begin interpreting their results. It has been said that data is a lot like garbage: You need to know what you are going to do with it before you start collecting it.

Yet leaders are unlikely to know what they want to know until they experiment. This work is a discovery process. It starts by wrestling with questions, and then testing the questions before rushing to make meaning.

To be clear, the first set of metrics from your questions may really be more helpful in rethinking better metrics than they are in providing helpful information for shifting the lag metric.

The question to wrestle with is: What do you want to know?

The *something* you are learning from your metrics may offer some faithful surprises or may illustrate an opportunity to redesign the metrics. Either result is a success.

Practical, administrative vs. deeply relational

From a faithful business perspective, there is great value in having metrics that point to the practical when managing a church. A metric that celebrates giving, focused on the congregational practice of generosity, for example, is an important indicator of the financial health of the congregation. It is also a spiritual health indicator of the maturity of the people in the congregation. Seeds of generosity are not automatically planted in people when they worship. People have to be taught to recognize that their gifts are essential to the sustainability of the ministry and to the practice of their own personal faith.

Metrics like these are similar to the yellow arrows and little shells in that they are purposeful and important. When naming metrics, lead metrics that shift the lag metric of the bottom line will be included in your final list. Examples of these lead metrics can be found at waytolead.org/metrics.

These metrics are crucial and faithful. They may encourage those with a mature, growing faith, or even stir up passion for a deepening faith life. Others, however, may be unmoved, and may long for something they interpret as *more spiritual*. Inspirational metrics will vary from person to person.

Metrics on the Camino de Santiago are like this as well. Yellow arrows are just yellow arrows. They point in the right direction. For many people, the confidence they feel when they see one of these arrows is life-giving as they are making their way on the path. Yet others will not find the arrows inspiring and instead focus on the new relationships they made on the journey.

The stamps in the passport are relational.

These indicators have more to do with the moments, the stories, and the people than the stamps themselves and encourage hearts on the journey.

Relational lead or lag metrics are gold. They are the sparks that get the fire going. If leaders want to shift the outcomes of lag metrics, attention to relational lead metrics will usually be the most effective. God works in people's lives through other people. Focus here.

As part of LEAD's research for this field guide, we interviewed a group of pastors younger than 40 to get their thoughts on relational metrics. Here are a few of the questions they offered as starting places for developing both lag and lead metrics:

⊕ How many kids are in worship vs. how many families send kids to Sunday school while the parents go to church?

⊕ If your church has a school or preschool, how many school families vs. how many church families participate in congregational events?

⊕ How does milestone attendance change over the year? For example, follow one class over the course of a number of years to watch how participation changes and grows.

⊕ How many failures can we celebrate as people take risks, trying new things?

⊕ How many hours do members spend volunteering with community organizations each month over a year?

⊕ How much time do grandparents spend with their grandchildren in prayer and faith formation, and how often?

- How much time do men spend with male friends outside of work and church, and how often?
- How many people are able to be vulnerable with each other in and out of worship?
- How many younger leaders are invited, stepping up, coached, and freed to serve?
- How many people have attempted, are in the process of, or have learned English or Spanish so they can have better relationships with other members?
- How many different people show up early for worship to help set up or stay after to tear down?
- How long do people stay after worship because they enjoy the relationships that are developing?
- What is the number of phone calls/texts/conversations centered around faith development and prayer outside of Sunday worship?
- How long does it take to turn to the correct chapter/verse in the Bible during Bible study and Sunday worship?
- How many people are engaged in small groups or seasonal devotions?
- How many parent conversations and engagements happen outside of Sunday morning?
- What is the number of new people who have transitioned into a higher level of leadership in the congregation during the year?
- What is the number of people who consider themselves mentors to someone else in the congregation?
- How often do people talk about or mention their church to people/friends outside the church?
- How many people know the congregation's purpose/mission/vision? How many know what the core values are?
- What is the parking lot capacity during the week? (Is the building being used?)
- How many neighbors/partners can identify your church?
- What percentage of the total budget is allocated for mission support?

Are their ideas prompting others in your imagination? Make your own list.

Think about this:
- Can you see the human connection in each of these lag or lead metrics?
- Can you imagine their meaning?
- Can you tell their stories?
- Can you brainstorm experiments?
- If they are lag metrics, can you identify a lead metric that will influence them?

Starting with this list and revisiting your previous notes will help you evaluate your own metrics. LEAD found metrics that support technical goals were easier to build. Adaptive, relational metrics, which are often more meaningful, took more thought. The rich conversations that come out of this process help grow trust, shared language, and commitment.

Understanding the metrics

Testing your metrics is key. Yet even with great sampling, you won't know what you are missing until you run the experiment. There is truth in the idea that you don't know what you don't know.

Whenever LEAD writes surveys, we wish we had asked different questions the minute people start answering them. Although we were thoughtful and purposeful in preparing the questions and even tested them before we used them, we are inevitably frustrated with the results. This is because when we do a survey, we are engaged in single-loop learning. Our questions get answers, but maybe not the ones we anticipated. There is an art to research!

Questions produce **Answers**

The answers themselves usually makes us want to ask more questions. Sometimes these are clarifying questions, but often they are completely different questions. Interpretation is weak unless we follow up to get more information. Using a first round of questions to drive a second more focused and generally deeper question is known as double-loop learning. The learning from the first (single) loop inspires more learning for another round (double-loop) of questions that drill down to discover more significant information.

Questions produce **Answers that produce**

More Questions that produce better Answers

Surveys and interviews are most effective when you take the set of questions raised by

the first round of listening and use those to revisit the data or, better yet, to ask new questions of the same people or people in the same situation.

Double-loop learning is worth the time it takes and is more likely to offer those aha moments you are seeking. It informs better metrics and increases the chance of desired results.

LEAD is made up of curious learners with a thirst for excellence. We are not professional researchers, but that doesn't stop us from digging into what we are observing.

However, when we are focused on a targeted area of interest, we often partner with professional researchers. We build our thinking on the incredible work done by social science researchers. Their work is foundational for all of our listening.

Yet, we are the quasi-experts who have the courage to ask our own questions and the commitment to carefully listen to our own clients. Because of our commitment and investment in focused listening over time, our learning has been significant.

Each time we return to listening, we move our best guess a little closer to the mark. Part of this process includes our increasing ability to identify our own blind spots, those things that effect our judgment.

The introduction to this field guide outlined one perspective of adult learning theory. The capacity to ask yourself better questions based on what you have learned, to draw more strategic conclusions, and to use that information in your behavior is all part of your own growth as adaptive leaders.

In their book, *The Practice of Adaptive Leadership: Tools and Tactics for Changing Your Organization and the World*, Heifetz, Grashow, and Linsky write:

> Adaptive leadership is an iterative process involving three key activities: 1) observing events and patterns around you; 2) interpreting what you are observing (developing a hypothesis about what is really going on); and 3) designing interventions based on the observations and interpretations to address the adaptive challenge you have identified. Each of these activities builds on the ones that come before it: and the process overall is iterative: you repeatedly refine your observations, interpretations, and interventions. (p. 32)

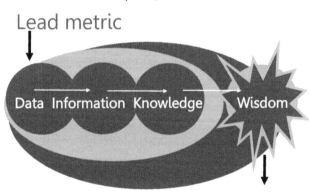

Why is double-loop learning so helpful?

Setting faithful metrics will produce data that gives leaders information and sometimes even knowledge. Knowledge is awareness that results from learning. Knowledge has been said to be power—but power for what?

To understand what the metrics are revealing, you need wisdom. This comes from experience and from testing the knowledge you acquire over time.

Leaders in the church have been prone to use their knowledge without wisdom to make costly decisions. Here are a few examples:

1. Metrics reveal fewer children in Sunday School.

    Knowledge suggests that parents aren't bringing their children because Sunday School is boring. The technical solution is better curriculum, better trained teachers, and nicer buildings.

    Wisdom, on the other hand, says that the issue is more complicated than this. Wisdom is informed by listening and research. You can fight to maintain Sunday School, an old technology for teaching the faith, or you can look at the research and listen to the people around you. Recognizing the role of caring adults in the faith of children and experimenting with new ministries are adaptive solutions.

    Wisdom can provide insight. While at first glance it may seem people no longer value spirituality and faith, this may not be the case. In this changing world, people are finding spirituality and faith everywhere. It is Sunday School that is in question. This is an important aha moment as it opens up opportunities to rethink how faith is taught.

Practicing faith within particular theological understandings matters to congregations. This is too important to ignore simply because one vehicle, Sunday School, may have run its course in some places.

2. Metrics reveal fewer people in worship.

Decreasing worship attendance, especially among young people, creates anxiety for congregations. Knowledge says that contemporary worship and PowerPoint projection are the answers (technical solutions).

Wisdom, on the other hand, reveals that people come because of their spiritual thirst for a relationship with God and other people. What may be understood as contemporary worship in some places has a different definition in others. Regardless, contemporary worship has not proven to be the answer to decreasing worship metrics.

You can experiment by listening to your neighbors so their voices influence how you reform worship to be more than a gathering in the sanctuary (adaptive solution).

Congregations that focus on relationships with God and each other are growing deeper in faith. It is integrated into a larger way of life, rooted in meaningful experiences of the sacred.

Rethinking these sacred cows is hard. Grief goes along with the journey toward wisdom as you let go of what has been most meaningful in the past. Some congregations embrace their heritage by continuing traditional worship while, at the same time, experimenting with other styles of worship.

Experiments, as already noted, may fail. Great learning can be gleaned from failure that, in turn, can inform the next experiment. This is part of the interpretation process.

Single-loop learning that offers knowledge is always stronger when it gives way to double-loop learning that creates deeper wisdom. The cycle of experimenting with lead metrics, interpreting what they are indicating, then returning for a second experiment is the work of adaptive leaders.

Managing the heat

As a reminder, congregations have varying bandwidths for change. The pace of change, the amount of change, and the frequency of change create heat in the system. According to Heifetz, Grashow, and Linsky[11], in *The Practice of Adaptive Leadership: Tools and Tactics for Changing Your Organization and*

Learn more: [11]Heifetz, Grashow and Linsky, *The Practice of Adaptive Leadership: Tools and Tactics for Changing Your Organization and the World the World*, it is the leader's job to manage the heat. Leadership has its hand on the thermostat determining how what is interpreted gets communicated in the congregation.

8. Discipleship

Are discipleship metrics possible?

For better or worse, the church is rooted in an ancient faith that has made it this far with faithful experiments. One of the strengths of Christian tradition is truths proven over time. Yet each interpretation of truth has taken different forms. Recognizing that what is measured gets reproduced and has influence, what kind of metrics would leaders dare suggest?

Five hundred years after the European Reformation, leaders give thanks to God for some of these gifts. Luther and the reformers before him can be credited for the Bible being translated into the language of the people and the technology of the printing press for liberating the gospel from the church in Rome. Christians are grateful for the theology of grace introducing the oppressed to a very different understanding of God than the God that had been presented in the church.

And at the same time, many Christians feel a deep sadness for what this has meant for non-Europeans who have long been victims of colonization. The voices of Native Americans and others should move Christians to confess that the freedom of the Reformation was not felt by everyone.

The words of Negro spirituals bring us to our knees with the pain they experienced at the hands of good Christians. Liberation theologians raise up human rights issues and point to God's preferential treatment of the poor. All of this sits in contrast to the past 50

years with the Christian right melding politics and the Christian faith.

People can and will do amazing and not-so-amazing things in the name of Jesus.

Gaining a faith-filled perspective

Scrolling back to the beginning of the Christian movement provides some perspective. Walking through the ruins of the early church in Turkey, Greece, and Rome, the risks that followers of Jesus must have taken can be imagined, but it takes a little decoding to make sense of the language in the Apostle Paul's letters. His words sound very different to 21st-century ears than they did to his intended audience of first century Christians.

Historians believe Paul's letters are the oldest record of Jesus' ministry as reflected in the early church. Even so, there was almost a generation between Jesus's death and resurrection and these written records. The Jesus movement was left in the hands of a ragtag army of fishermen, tax collectors, and women, all gifted with the power of the Holy Spirit.

The point here is that church leaders in the past have done the best they can, but the past isn't perfect. Their missing the mark should, at the very least, provide the courage to lead. After all, if leaders are inspired by the deep faith and willingness to risk of those who went before, but choose not step up now, they are missing their call.

Leaders take chances. They ask new questions and explore what God is doing now. This is Christian leadership at its best. If any metrics matter, measures for discipleship must be on the list—or what is the point of the church?

The only thing that makes the church different from any other nonprofit organization is the conviction that God loves people in spite of themselves, that God is pouring out grace through Jesus Christ, and that the Holy Spirit lives and works in all people, at all times. (Yes, this is a simplification.) If congregations spend all their time measuring the same things that other nonprofits focus on without bothering to set metrics that are faith based, why do they exist? Isn't this missing the point?

If this invitation to measure discipleship feels totally awkward, theologically unsound, and personally unfaithful, is it still worth doing?

LEAD believes the answer is yes. Open your mind and reflect on this idea for a few minutes.

If what is measured gets reproduced, then shouldn't metrics be focused on faith? Isn't it your call, with the power of the Holy Spirit, to share the Gospel with the world?

Jesus provided great examples of metrics. They are everywhere in the Bible once you get comfortable with this way of thinking. The New Testament is filled with parables and healing stories describing discipleship. Begin by reflecting on Matthew 25:34-40.

 Then the king will say to those at his right hand, 'Come, you that are blessed by my Father, inherit the kingdom prepared for you from the foundation of the world; for I was hungry and you gave me food, I was thirsty and you gave me something to drink, I was a stranger and you welcomed me, I was naked and you gave me clothing, I was sick and you took care of me, I was in prison and you visited me.' Then the righteous will answer him, 'Lord, when was it that we saw you hungry and gave you food, or thirsty and gave you something to drink? And when was it that we saw you a stranger and welcomed you, or naked and gave you clothing? And when was it that we saw you sick or in prison and visited you?' And the king will answer them, 'Truly I tell you, just as you did it to one of the least of these who are members of my family, you did it to me.'

Do lead metrics for discipleship jump out at you when you read this text? Are you getting the picture that discipleship includes these four imperatives and more?
⊕ Feeding the hungry
⊕ Welcome the stranger
⊕ Clothing the naked

⊕ Caring for the sick
⊕ Visiting those in prison

Single-loop knowledge says that these are not metaphors. Advocating and responding to the needs of others changes their lives. Christians are a people who respond to human need and suffering in the name of Jesus the Christ. Leaders could spend a lifetime focusing on these four practices, and making technical changes that improve the ways leaders live out this text.

Double-loop wisdom reveals more. Investing in the care of others changes the lives of those giving the care too. Loop back through this scripture with new questions like:

What happens in people's lives when they:
⊕ feed the hungry?
⊕ welcome the stranger?
⊕ clothe the naked?
⊕ care for the sick?
⊕ visit those in prison?

What is the relationship between the seven Congregational Practices and these mandates?

Applying double-loop learning to this text, in tension with your best thinking, is a great way to test decisions.

Putting these two lists side by side raises important questions about the impact of outward ministry. Notice how the metrics from Matthew 25 drive God's people outward, into relationships with people whose lives are filled with grief and pain. This is a push into discomfort that is overflowing with unmeasurable blessings.

Matthew 25:34-40	7 Congregational Practices
Feeding the hungry	Worship, Partnership
Welcome the stranger	Worship, Leadership, Community, Care, Partnership
Visiting those in prison	Spirituality
Caring for the sick	Community, Care
Clothing the naked	Generosity, Leadership

Could this be why people of faith pour out their resources every time there is a natural disaster? A tidal wave of love rises up in tragedy, giving evidence to a deep desire to care and to give. There is room for deeper conversations about the way people give, the kind of stuff they give, and the opportunities to influence giving so that what is really needed is provided. Yet this compassionate response is an indicator of *something* worth asking more questions about.

The Christian church in Africa is growing faster than anywhere else on earth. These brothers and sisters demonstrate how to live in community in ways that have been forgotten by the institutionalized church. Based on Matthew 25, is it any wonder that these churches are focused on building hospitals and schools, empowering leaders, and fighting malaria?

When faith in Jesus drives people out of themselves, everything changes. People do amazing things when they are part of communities that are being Christ in the world.

From the beginning of this field guide, we have emphasized that each congregation has to create its own metrics. LEAD does offer a digital dashboard and consulting, but the point of these resources is to help congregations discern God's call. Expertise in crucial areas that build on the existing stakeholders in your congregation is available. We believe God is at work in everyone.

Read the Bible with curiosity—what is God calling you to pay attention to? What does discipleship look like on your watch?

Paying attention to discipleship leaves less time to spend on micromanaging protocols that have outlived their day. Use the discipline of faithful metrics to support behavior shifts. LEAD's work in congregations the past few years has shown that this is possible.

We are not suggesting that discipleship be reduced to a formula. A deepening faith life is so much more contagious than a program. Faithful metrics can encourage strategic experiments with the potential for life-changing meaning. It's about focus and alignment that result in transformation.

A true story of discipleship and metrics

One congregation LEAD has partnered with is located on a large piece of property within a low-income community. As a longtime gardener, the pastor secretly wondered about starting a community garden. The power systems in the congregation made her feel that this would not be welcomed by many of the older members and so the idea and the land sat dormant. Every time she cautiously proposed the idea to a leader, questions about liability and risks brought the conversation to a halt. The pastor's apprehension for leading this vision grew.

After some discernment by the congregation's leadership, a goal was set to join other congregations in a learning cohort and engage in the LEAD Tune In Process. Eight months into the experience, after listening in the neighborhood, food insecurity rose up as a high concern. The pastor took a risk and shared her vision of a community garden. She told the rest of the story with tears in her eyes.

The congregation's team took a chance. They brought the vision of a small garden to the council who reluctantly agreed to it. The story continues to unfold as obstacle after obstacle has been overcome.

⊕ The congregation had no tools, but an unexpected grant provided funding for them.

⊕ The soil needed improving; someone at a nearby farm had more compost than they could use, so they delivered a few truckloads at no cost.

⊕ The water source was not near the plot of land, but a landscaper in the community offered to put in an irrigation system at cost.

⊕ They had no seeds, but someone on the city council told them about another nonprofit's free seed program.

⊕ They didn't know as much about gardening as they wished they did, so the local agricultural program helped.

⊕ They only had a handful of workers, but the neighbors showed up to help.

⊕ They had more harvest than they could use in the local neighborhood, so they donated to the food pantry.

The congregation's team never saw this coming. Their lag metric was to connect to their neighborhood. Their lead metric was to build a community garden. It was a home run. Today they are planning for the second season of this adventure. The planning team is a partnership of congregational members and the neighborhood. And some people in the congregation are still unhappy about the garden.

I was hungry and you gave me something to eat.

The adaptive leadership in this congregation continues to grow. This story is just beginning and the possibilities are ripe for exploring.

The lead metric has successfully shifted their lag metric. They are wondering what is next.

As you wonder if it is faithful to set metrics that deepen discipleship, you have to also wonder what it means to be disciples.

Knowledge almost always points to a technical fix. The hard work of double-loop learning will reveal wisdom that inspires adaptive experiments. The uncertainty of leading in a changing world may make you yearn for the tried and true ways of the past even as you recognize that they are less and less effective. The Holy Spirit is inviting leaders to discern wisdom for a new season of church, and faithful metrics can help.

This is a process, not a program.

Leaders looking for a quick fix will find this process slower than they would like because the perfect lead metric is seldom identified on the first try. In addition, just when you think the lead metric is working, something in the larger context will shift reality. Natural disasters, for example, wreak havoc with what has been seen as normal, throwing all metrics out of balance. This may be a temporary speed bump or the end of life as you knew it.

Faithful metrics are never "one and done." Each season brings with it the opportunity to reevaluate the metrics themselves.

Camouflaging truth

It is worth noting that the processes of single- and double-loop learning can reveal hot spots that leaders have been hiding over the years. It is not unusual for a closer look at

congregational systems to reveal some less-than-honorable decision making or organizational practices, or survival techniques that are out of date, left over from previous generations of leaders.

This is especially painful if it exposes a beloved pastor or longtime member and elder of the community. The big decision for today's leaders is how much camouflage they will use.

It is unhelpful to:
⊕ Hide the truth to spare past saints. Truth-telling is crucial to building an ethical future. Misconduct that involves financial mismanagement or abuse of power in a sexual relationship must be confronted. Small managerial errors, where it is clear people were doing the best they could without violating ethics, should be corrected with the least amount of harm to the relationships.
⊕ Create new smoke screens to cover old sins. Hiding truth is worse than sharing it, even if short-term discomfort accompanies the bad news. Never add to the problem by sweeping more under the rug.
⊕ Use past sins to throw leaders under the bus rather than take up the hard work of today's leadership. Shaming previous generations of leaders who may have interpreted situations differently is not helpful either. Moving forward can mean offering grace to humans who were doing their best in a different season of the church.

In most cases, making the hard decision to tell the truth in love without trashing relationships will strengthen the ministry over time. Leaders are wise to remember that each season of leadership has its challenges.

A diminished view of past seasons of leadership never serves the future.

Returning to the work of Brené Brown, discussed in Chapter 1, provides a reminder that, in general, people are doing the best they can.

Using double-loop learning, leaders can do their own self-evaluation as they set metrics for future results, *doing the best they can*. God has used imperfect leaders throughout time to tell the world of God's love.

It is your turn to interpret and reinterpret ministry and mission through this love God has for the world, for your neighborhood, your congregation, your family and yourself. As an agent of this love, you can tell the stories that will move the mission forward and give the whole community courage to be God's people in a changing world.

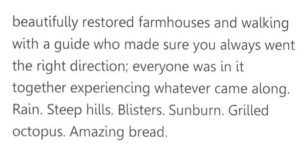

9. Movement

POV is short for point of view.

Everyone has one, or maybe more than one, as you'll see in the discussion of intersectionality later in this chapter.

What surprised us most about the general POV on the Camino was an unspoken understanding that everyone's Camino was valid. It didn't matter if you had walked out of your front door in Germany three months ago and slept in tents or in albergues (hostels filled with bunk beds in spaces shared by men and women) or if you had just joined the pilgrimage and were staying in

beautifully restored farmhouses and walking with a guide who made sure you always went the right direction; everyone was in it together experiencing whatever came along. Rain. Steep hills. Blisters. Sunburn. Grilled octopus. Amazing bread.

We were in a weird little alternate universe where the journey really was more important than anything else.

This mutual respect rolled into our faith lives as well. The Camino is peppered with relics of ancient churches. If you take time to go inside them, you will encounter artifacts of a very different spirituality than most current pilgrims embrace. Just because it

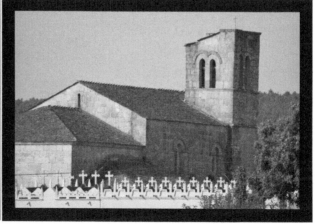

wasn't *your* tradition didn't mean you would walk on by. Rather, you might find yourself standing in line to get into tiny little stone buildings or larger more ornate structures. God was universal, in the best sense of the word.

This universal God-view was helpful, considering all the different POVs on the path. The word pilgrim is not exclusive to any denomination. It does not imply a specific belief system, but it does put you on a spiritual quest surrounded by an ocean of humanity.

As we walked, our group was immersed in reading the book of Ruth. We entered into our pilgrimage through the stories of two women making their way in life together. We felt growing appreciation for Naomi who, in her grief and poverty, agreed to take her Moabite refugee daughter-in-law with her when she returned to her family.

Studying scripture in community made a difference in our relationship with each other. As our relationship with God grew, so did our trust with each other.

It worked for us. We journaled. Prayed. Sang.

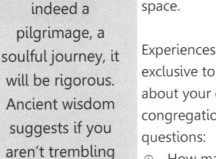

If your journey is indeed a pilgrimage, a soulful journey, it will be rigorous. Ancient wisdom suggests if you aren't trembling as you approach the sacred, it isn't the real thing. The sacred, in its various guises as holy ground, art, or knowledge, evokes emotion and commotion.
Phil Cousineau
The Art of Pilgrimage

We felt free to be in relationship with each other and with God without any other expectation. This freedom moved us to share our faith questions without fear of being shamed.

As we walked, deep God-stories that had seldom been told came into the light, making it a healing space.

Experiences like these are not exclusive to the Camino. Think about your own family or congregation as you consider these questions:
⊕ How many God moments are people naming each week?
⊕ How many spaces or places that foster vulnerability are available each month?
⊕ How often do people feel free to ask their heartfelt God questions?

Staying on course

Most people follow the yellow arrows or the images of the shell to confirm they are on the right path while walking the Camino. Some of us contracted with guides who shared both their knowledge of the Camino and their leadership on the road.

The guides made sure we didn't follow any false arrows. Not surprisingly, some small business owners wanting to drive foot traffic their way took people off the official Camino by strategically placing yellow arrows. These could result in walking much farther than planned, getting lost, or getting distracted from the pilgrimage.

The guides also made sure we saw ancient ruins, unique landscapes, or special churches we would have otherwise missed. This often meant adding more distance to the journey— but it was purposeful.

The accompaniment of people who knew the way on the Camino was a true gift to the experience. Not unlike LEAD's coaches or consultants, the guides helped us get the most out of the journey. They freed us from worry so we could focus on our relationship with God and with one another.

Choose your relational frame carefully as it can shape point of view for generations.

Intersection, integration and intersectionality

These God stories reflect the intersections of our relationship with God and with each other. The word intersection is very useful when talking about data and relationships. It moves information from silos to a synergistic work-cultural wholeness.

It is important to note here that LEAD intentionally chose not to use the word "integration." Integration devalues human beings by stereotyping language, skin color, ethnicity, gender, or sexual identity and is outside of our understanding of faith. In doing so, the fullness of who people are as individuals and communities is not accounted for. This is outside our understanding of faith.

A quick glance at US History is helpful here as an example of how what may begin as good intentions can have unexpected consequences.

The massive effort to desegregate public schools across the United States was a major goal of the civil rights movement. This grew out of concerns in the education system, that separate was not equal and that every child, regardless of race, deserved a first-class education.

These lawsuits were combined into the *Brown v. Board of Education* Supreme Court case that outlawed segregation in schools in 1954. But the vast majority of segregated schools were not integrated until many years later. As important as this legislation was for equal access to quality education, there are many who think this had very little positive impact on integrating relationships across cultures. There are people in this country, in various racial groups, that hold to the values of this legislation, and at the same time recognize the important relational work is largely unfinished.

Integration, without a full understanding of what it takes to form relationships, can devalue the very people it attempts to support. For this reason, LEAD is committed to the concept of intersection.

Intersection is reflected both within and between individuals. Let's begin by considering intersection within an individual.

As Rozella White writes in LEAD's *Work Out Guide*, "to be human is to a be living, breathing, relational intersection." (p. 44)

Each individual is an intersection of multiple identities in relationship with each other. Your ability to be open to potential innovative power deepens if you first understand the various parts that make up who you are and come to terms with the meaning that each part holds. This understanding of the richness of a person's identity is known as intersectionality.

Intersectional Theory, the idea that our identity is made up of various intersections that inform all of who we are, was first coined in 1989 by Kimberlé Williams Crenshaw, an American civil rights advocate and leading scholar of critical race theory. Her work gives definition to the reality of overlapping or intersecting social identities and related systems of oppression, domination or discrimination. The theory proposes that we think of each element or trait of a person as inextricably linked with all of the other elements in order to fully understand our identity.

> Let us confess our sin in the presence of God and of one another.
> God of overflowing grace, we come to you with repentant hearts.
> *Evangelical Lutheran Worship*

According to Intersectional Theory, in order to understand the whole of a person, the various parts that make up that person and the meaning that those parts have within society must be understood.

People are not somehow separate or apart from the systems and influences that govern their lives. Intersectional Theory provides a way of knowing one's self in a way that can deepen your engagement with neighbors and within your community.

The more leaders learn from Intersectionality theory, the better they can interpret data, metrics, and relationships for transformation. This POV is an intentional shift for Christians; it will not happen if leaders are on autopilot, doing what they have always done before.

Intersectionality impacts the stories that are shared to give life to metrics. It impacts relationships with God and with each other.

While integration is often used in the context of data, it cannot be used in a congregation's stories or to unpack a congregation's metrics. Words shape culture. In the end, integration will work against the outcomes of a faithful congregation. Grasping this is important.

This is a good place to push pause on your reading and use these questions for personal and group conversation:
What are the creative, life-giving intersections in your personal life?

⊕ Have fun with this. Think about intersection like peanut butter and chocolate.
⊕ Get serious about this. Think about intersection like parents and teenagers.
⊕ Connect faith and life. Think about intersection like walking or running and prayer.
⊕ Go deeper with this. Think about intersection like people with different points of view.
⊕ Be relational about this. Think about intersection like two people falling in love.
⊕ Get personal about this. What are the intersecting realities that make you who you are? How are those realities viewed by others? By society? How might this impact how you understand yourself and others?
⊕ What else can you think of?

In the words of Marlon Hall[12], "There is no innovation without intersection."

Staying on course with metric intersections

Just as the yellow arrows kept us on the Camino, or alerted us to intentional detours, metrics can provide similar guidance.

Congregations have multiple intersections that can be crucial for effective alignment.

Leaders can loose site of values and purpose when internal pressures from fragile relationships factor in to the conversation. intentional alignment of both vertical Intersections and horizontal intersections are crucial to staying the course.

Vertical intersection involves the connection between God's mission and how it is lived out in the congregation's purpose and core values. There is alignment between what is measured and the direction God is calling the congregation to ministry in the world.

Horizontal intersection is the connection of metrics across the congregation that ensure teamwork, building trust, and deepening relationships with each other, neighbors, or visitors.

Ministry leaders who work in silos get disconnected. Congregations of any size can discover that some ministry areas are aligned within shared metrics, while others are actually, if unintentionally, working against the shared metrics.

Metrics can be effectively captured on dashboards with incremental growth, yet not lead in a faithful direction. Distractions from values and purpose are pervasive, often reflecting a lack of intersection. For example, if one value of *Brown v. Board of Education* included integrating black and white children

Learn more: [12]Marlon Hall, The Awakenings Movement

(or families) then the bussing strategy missed the mark.

LEAD has seen congregations change the language of youth ministry to family ministry, indicating a value shift, without changing the historic internal lag metric of "how many youth came on Sunday night?" This change is especially challenging if the leadership is successfully supporting ministry in the home, possibility on Sunday night. An intentional horizontal intersection could include greater attention to the voices of the youth, parents, and families in the congregation and neighborhood than to people for whom youth group was a meaningful past experience.

LEAD has also seen congregations commission a team of leaders to create a strategic plan that includes an aspirational value of hospitality, with lag metrics of increasing worship attendance, internal technical goals for adding signage, welcome gifts, etc. without the deeper, adaptive work of preparing people to talk with people they don't know. Yet when the lag metric does not change dramatically, people feel discouraged because their technical efforts did not produce their hoped-for results. Imagine the difference if the leaders listened to the neighbors to discover their hunger for spirituality, so this could factor into a strong horizontal intersection.

Finally, one last example LEAD sees often is the disconnect between the values of a congregation and the budget. Imagine if a congregation's values, goals, and budget

formed a fully vertical and horizontal intersection.

All of these examples could be interpreted a variety of ways. Yet imagine the outcomes if a fuller alignment with attention to the multiple intersections that are part of each example were part of the conversation.

Full intersection is seldom achieved, but a good measurement system functions best when key leaders, including staff (paid or unpaid) and the church council, are on the same page.

Worksheets and stories of congregations working to create both vertical and horizontal intersection can be found at waytolead.org/metrics.

A word of caution and the congregations God-narrative

We chose to use the word "intersection" to describe the relationship between metrics and the practices of teams, committees, and staffs. This is also helpful as it applies to our intersection with our faith life.

This attention to point of view matters more than you realize.

Congregations have a God-narrative that may be keeping people stuck in their own small world thinking. If leaders are not careful, they can gather data to reinforce metrics and tell stories that ultimately work against the true mission of the church. This is where it is necessary to engage your theological lens with intentionality.

For clarity on the mission of the church, look past your own worldview to Jesus's teachings in the Sermon on the Mount or observe his life of inclusivity, hospitality, and meaningful relationships.

A reality check

As you make meaning out of metrics, ask yourself:

⊕ If people actually live into the future described in the metrics, what does this mean for their relationships?

⊕ How will the mindsets of those already in the congregation need to grow in order to be open to what God is doing?

⊕ What may have to stop happening in the congregation?

⊕ What may have to start happening?

⊕ What is the role of congregational leaders in spiritually accompanying these shifts?

⊕ What stories might be told now that could make a way forward?

⊕ What data collection would help shape the path ahead?

Digital and congregational echo chamber alert

The over-connected digital world of today reinforces relationships among people who are similar to one another. Digital bubbles are created to block out the noise and distractions all around. They can lead us to believe everyone things like we do.
This becomes dangerous when a

congregation serves as an echo chamber for a single point of view. In many ways, this is the paradigm that *Faithful Metrics* is working to move beyond during this time of opportunity and change.

The echo chamber as a way of living out congregational life has run its course. We live in a diverse, fast-changing, dynamic, inter-connected world. Things are not going back to the way they used to be. The new normal looks more like a whirlwind of innovation and creativity than it does status quo. Adaptive leadership is the only leadership that will thrive in the whirlwind.

The next season of faith life will look more inclusive, more open to diversity, and more friendly to people we have not met yet. This will not happen instantly or automatically. Resistance will not stop this change from happening. Yet the church is not a victim of this whirlwind either.

Leaders have to pave the way for new behaviors and practices. The metrics you select, the stories you tell about these metrics, the language you use and the relationships they inform will be part of the journey. The pilgrimage will have hot spots that can be managed and some that will blister before they heal. Managing the heat is truly the work of leadership.

The church's history includes a prophetic voice. It also includes times of being stalled with an insulated, closed mindset. Jesus modeled a life of faith that embraced and even sought out diversity. This call to diversity is embedded in a faithful call to discipleship and should be evident in your metrics.

As you move toward identifying your congregation's metrics, it is your responsibility to address this echo chamber. Ask yourself:

⊕ Will we perpetuate a stalled, closed mindset or will we use this as an opportunity to open up the faith community so it can grow beyond itself?

⊕ What is the POV our metrics, stories, and relationships will use to join God in mission in this changing world?

Three final thoughts to summarize this chapter, before taking the next step on the Camino:

⊕ Alignment is not single-mindedness. It is possible for a community to hold together around shared values and at the same time welcome very diverse people.

⊕ Metrics have vertical and horizontal intersections. Attention to God moving in the congregation (vertical) and God moving in the neighborhood and world (horizontal) are both important.

⊕ Intersection is not intersectionality. The identity of individuals and of the congregation are multi-layered and interconnected.

Faithful metrics free people to be who they are. Because of what Christ did on the cross and what the Holy Spirit is doing right now, everyone's POV is valid. It doesn't get better than that.

Conclusion

Hard questions ahead

When we reached our destination, Santiago de Compostela was full of people celebrating at a festival in the square. We had to wait our turn to put our feet on the "finish line" and then wait in line to get into the cathedral. The place was packed with pilgrims from around the world, all converging for mass. We squeezed into this sacred space and, with no seats left, most of us ended up on the floor to rest our tired feet. Everything was in Spanish (since this was Spain, of course!), yet we could understand the rhythm of the worship service. The space was congested; a mass of humanity crowded into the enormous, opulent cathedral, all feeling the energy of the celebration—a pilgrimage completed! Very emotional. Very meaningful. Very moving.

And then, in English came these words: UNLESS YOU ARE IN GOOD STANDING WITH THE ROMAN CATHOLIC CHURCH YOU ARE NOT WELCOMED AT THIS TABLE.

Bam! The door was slammed and most of the people in the room, the pilgrims, were pushed out. It just felt so ... *wrong ... in this place*.

We exchanged glances with each other, ready to walk out. But we were stuck in the crowded room without an easy exit. Worship had ended for us at that point. DONE.

As we left at the end of the service, it was as if the very spirit of the place had shifted for those of us who were not welcomed at the table. Although we didn't really talk about it, anger was rising up within our group. A silent anger.

Later that night we gathered for dinner in a special room that had been prepared for our group of 12. As the wine and the bread were served, our eyes met again.

The body of Christ, broken for you.
The blood of Christ, shed for you.

The words were spoken and the gifts were passed from person to person.

As the bread and the wine moved away from me, I felt our guide Olga's eyes on me. She looked at me like a hungry child, and said, "Can I do it? Can I take the communion?" Then the table got very quiet as she said, "I've never done it. I'm not baptized. Can I do it tonight?"

I looked at her. I looked at the group. I know the church polity. But in that moment, I said, and I meant it, "Olga, everyone is welcomed at this table."

There wasn't a dry eye at the table when she received the gifts for the first time.

What would you do at a time like this?

Leaders will always face crucible moments when they have to decide what will win the day. As you lead through the opportunities a changing world provides, your values, polity, and understanding of what matters most will be continually tested.

Reflecting on the history of the church can illustrate times when leaders opened the door wider or when access to the church became exclusively available to only a select group of people. Even a fast read of the book of Acts will illustrate the challenge that the early church faced with these same questions.

Can the uncircumcised "get in?" What about the eunuch (Acts 8)? The Centurion (Acts 10)?

Today you sit in this sacred space wielding leadership authority that stretches your best thinking beyond reason. How you measure, the stories you tell as you interpret metrics, and the point of view you take on God moving in your midst must be prayerfully tended.

Metrics produce *something*. What is the faithful something that the leadership in your congregation will stake its life on? If faith in a living God is not worth more than institutional survival or pleasing the biggest givers, then you are not leaders. Management is stewarding the resources you have been given. Leadership is taking risks to build on those resources for something bigger than any one individual and any congregation.

Pivot or persevere

LEAD uses the language "pivot or persevere" because it creates space to ask hard questions. Leaders must be constantly asking themselves if this is a time to pivot (go in a new direction) or persevere (keep going in the same direction). In either case, the prayer is that the decisions and ministry choices made are faithful responses to joining in God's mission.

Faithful metrics grow out of hearts in prayer. They illustrate your God-narrative and shape your practice of church. You care about how many people show up because you know showing up matters. You care about how much money people give because everything belongs to God and generosity is a faith practice. Yet this resource illustrates that an over-focus on these important lag metrics has been part of a loss of vision for God's mission.

LEAD is committed to learning what lead metrics move your congregation forward. There is no single set of metrics worth mass producing, yet there are some outward lead metrics, with vertical and horizontal alignment, that can help leaders discover the path forward.

You are indeed leading on a faithful pilgrimage with a new road ahead. Behaviors of the past run the risk of becoming obstacles for the future. Now is the time to start experimenting your way forward with confidence that God is with you on this journey.

In summary

This field guide has captured a lot of technical and adaptive work in one resource. It is not a how-to book, but a conversation for leaders walking on their own pilgrimage. There will be new learnings, stories, and

tweaks along the way. While the key parts of this journey are not necessarily new, this alignment for congregational life is a new way forward.

It is LEAD's prayer that by launching a metrics conversation, you and your congregation will wrestle with the larger questions of faith that drive deeply into the sacred. May God use your metrics, stories, and perspective to enrich the lives of the people around you, both those you know and those you are yet to know, for the sake of God's mission.

Glossary of Terms used in Faithful Metrics

Adaptive change
Problem solving that requires organizations or individuals to do things they have never done before. This means moving off the map to challenge their deeply held beliefs and values for the purpose of growth. Adaptive change is necessary for true growth and innovation.

Camino de Santiago
The Camino de Santiago is a network of paths leading to the shrine of the apostle Saint James the Great located in the Cathedral of Santiago de Compostela in Galicia, Spain. Tradition has it that the remains of the saint are buried there. Many pilgrims from across the world follow its routes as a way to grow a deeper spirituality.

Church
A gathering of believers. Church is not limited to a specific space, nor is it defined by the number of people gathered.

Congregation
A community of people working out their faith and life together, gathered with intention to grow deeper in their faith in God, their relationships with each other, and the world around them.

Core Values
Core values are the ideas at the center of an individual or organization's belief system. Once core values are defined, every decision should align with these values. LEAD understands that congregations have three different kinds of core values operating at the same time. These are Core Beliefs (Biblical, theological perspectives), Core Convictions (priorities for congregational life), and Core Practices (the primary activities of the ministry that align with Core Convictions and Core Beliefs).

Congregational Purpose
The reason a congregation exists. This provides the intention behind a congregation's decisions and actions. Congregational purpose should be shaped by the congregation's core values.

Culture
A collection of knowledge, experiences, values, beliefs, and attitudes shared by a group of people. Culture is at the core of an individual's worldview. It influences language, behaviors, traditions, manners, notions of time, spatial relations, and communication. Culture is a learned experience.

Dashboard

This is a progress report to collect data, that can provide a snapshot of your ministry.

Disciple

A follower of Christ actively wrestling with the question, "How can I live out my faith in the world?"

Diversity

A value or ethic that places high priority on including voices from a wide variety of perspectives. This includes considering race and ethnicity, gender, sexuality identity and expression, socioeconomic status, age, region, faith, education, and political persuasion. Creating space where a variety of views are not only welcome, but where power is shared, and leaders have actively sought out the perspectives of those not represented.

Double-loop

This learning model uses the a modification of answers to drive new questions in light of experience. When a problem is presented and an answer is given, the answer can be used to delve deeper into the problem by asking new questions that lead to deeper learning, providing more meaningful answers.

Ethnicity

An affiliation with a particular group tied to an individual's national or cultural tradition and identity.

Excellence

Deciding that it is not enough to accept the status quo or just "get it done." Excellence demands that leaders work at the highest level possible, even when it is uncomfortable, in order to earn quality results.

Frame

A frame is a lens intentionally applied to a situation to help make decisions. Frames are often proactive. For example, a person may choose to view a situation through the frame of a specific scripture passage or set of guidelines.

Gender

A social construct that defines the differences between male and female. Social scientists understand gender as a spectrum rather than as two opposite ideals. Gender can be tied to biological sex but often is separate. Gender norms, relationships, and roles are socially driven and vary from culture to culture. Individuals who do not identify with a culture's traditional gender norms may experience stigma or ostracism.

Intersectionality

Intersectionality was born out of the black feminist movement, an effort for black women concerned with equity to say that their femaleness and their blackness could not be understood separate and apart from each other. Identity is not enough. We as people of faith must dive deeper in our own understanding of how the various forces around us give meaning to identities—good, bad, or indifferent. We are not somehow separate or apart from the systems and influences that govern our lives. Intersectional Theory offers us a way of knowing that can deepen our engagement with our neighbors and within our community.

Lag metrics

Lag metrics measure something that has already happened by the time you get the data. At this point, there is nothing you can do to change the outcome. These indicators are largely output oriented. They are the result of lead metrics when used intentionally.

Lead metrics

Lead metrics are indicators that leaders strategically set, that have the potential to change the lag metric. They are predictive indicators that help shape a path forward. Lead metrics focus on process and define preemptive actions that lead to specific goals. These can be difficult to measure but are a key part of building a strategy for growth, particularly when used in combination with lag metrics.

Leader

Every individual has the ability to be a leader. Leaders exert influence in one or more areas of their life. Leaders may be the most outspoken people in a group but are equally likely to be quiet and thoughtful. Leadership can be taught and leaders are constantly learning.

Level up

A phrase meaning to work hard, increase or expand the capacity and impact of your leadership or your organization's influence in a particular context.

Metrics

A method of measurement. Metrics assign values to the goals of a project. Every project should have clear goals and outcome expectations that can be measured in some way. By clearly defining the metrics at the outset, it becomes easy to measure the success of a project and to see the ways in which it can be improved.

Mindset

A mindset is not fixed. Individuals and groups can move between a closed mindset, one that does not allow space for change, and a growth mindset from which an organization can thrive.

Neighbor

LEAD calls congregations and individuals to understand their neighbors both locally and globally. This means getting to know the people in your immediate area, those who can walk to your meeting place, as well as holding a constant awareness of the global connectivity of our world.

Pilgrim

A person who embarks on a spiritual journey with the understanding that the process matters more than the destination. A pilgrim believes that the sacred is found everywhere, not exclusively in a church setting, and actively seeks experiences that allow his or her faith to grow as a result of the journey.

Pilgrimage

A pilgrimage is a journey that calls a person to enter into liminal space where he or she expects God to act and expects to be different because of God. If Christians truly believe and live out the Resurrection and a theology of God's amazing grace, we can move beyond a faith focused on salvation to a faith grounded in how we live each day. A pilgrimage includes traveling with others, particularly those with diverse views and lifestyles; understanding that all life is sacred; and living in community with a high regard for others encountered along the journey.

Sexuality

Sexuality is the combination of an individual's gender identity, sexual orientation, and gender roles. Individuals may define their own sexuality.

Single-loop

This learning model is asking questions to get answers. Once you have the answer, you continue to use it as that problem's solution. (See Double-loop learning for a fuller process.)

Stakeholders

A person who has invested in an organization, idea, or practice. Stakeholders can help move an organization forward by investing in growth as defined by a leader or they can slow change by rejecting forward movement. A strong leader will work to build support with the organization's stakeholders. If the stakeholders lend support, the community will usually follow.

Technical change

Problem solving with a clear solution that ultimately reinstates the status quo. Technical change may ask organizations to alter details or goals but do not require challenging fundamental systems or beliefs.

Tune In

The Tune In Process is LEAD's ten-step program undertaken by a congregation to listen to God in scripture and prayer, in the congregation, and out in the neighborhood. A Listening Team guides the process, which includes periods of active listening followed by reflection. This process is intended to help congregations connect with their neighborhood through intentional listening.

Wake Up

The Wake Up Process is an effort to more fully align our own lives and our congregation's life with God's mission. A Centering Team guides this 10-step program drawing on ancient Christian prayer practices, faithful discernment, and strategic thinking to clarify congregational core values and purpose in alignment with God's mission. It's about missional identity formation.

Work Out

The Work Out Process is a 10-step program undertaken by a congregation to accompany leaders as they deepen their theological understanding, expand relationships beyond their comfort zones, and recognize the gifts, resources, assets, and humanity of all people. A Connecting Team will lead the process in the congregation by first moving through the steps themselves and then preparing to lead others in small groups through the Work Out Experience.

Worldview

A way of looking at the world that is informed by life experiences. This shapes an individual's reaction to a given situation. For example, a person's childhood, language, country of origin, and travel experience effect the way that person views the world.

Bibliography

Introduction:

Change Your Questions, Change Your Life: 10 Powerful Tools for Life and Work. Adams, Marilee

The Spirit of Youth and Culture of Youth Ministry: Leading Congregations Toward Exemplary Youth Ministry. Martinson, Roland

Leadership Agility: Five Levels of Mastery for Anticipating and Initiating Change. Joiner, Bill and Josephs, Stephen

Action Inquiry: The Secret of Timely and Transforming Leadership. Torbert, William R.

The Evolving Self and *In Over Our Heads: The Mental Demands of Modern Life.* Kegan, Robert

Spiral Dynamics: Mastering Values, Leadership and Change. Beck, Don and Cowan, Chris

Section One:

Rising Strong. Brown, Brené

New Revised Standard Version Bible, 1989

Evangelical Lutheran Worship, 2006

Chapter 1:

New Revised Standard Version Bible, 1989

Chapter 2:

Generations to Generations: Family Process in Church and Synagogue. Friedman, Edwin

The Practice of Adaptive Leadership: Tools and Tactics for Changing Your Organization and the World. Heifetz, Ronald, Grashow, Alexander and Linsky, Marty

Chapter 3:

Identity: Conversations with Benedetto Vecchi. Bauman, Zygmunt

The Missional Church in Perspective: Mapping Trends and Shaping the Conversation. Van Gelder, Craig and Zscheile, Dwight

Missional Renaissance: Changing the Scorecard for the Church. McNeal, Reggie

New Revised Standard Version Bible, 1989

Section Two:

Scaling Up: How a Few Companies Make It ... and Why the Rest Don't. Harnish, Verne

Chapter 4:

Evangelical Lutheran Worship, 2006

The Scattering: Imagining a Church that Connects Faith and Life. DuBois, Dwight

The Paradox of Generosity: Giving We Receive, Grasping We Lose. Smith, Christian and Hilary Davidson

Chapter 5:

The Power of Moments: Why Certain Experiences Have Extraordinary Impact. Heath, Dan and Heath, Chip

Chapter 6:

The Practice of Adaptive Leadership: Tools and Tactics for Changing Your Organization and the World. Heifetz, Ronald, Grashow, Alexander and Linsky, Marty

Section Three:

Chapter 7:

The Practice of Adaptive Leadership: Tools and Tactics for Changing Your Organization and the World. Heifetz, Ronald, Grashow, Alexander and Linsky, Marty

Chapter 8:

New Revised Standard Version Bible, 1989

Chapter 9:

The Art of Pilgrimage: A Seeker's Guide to Making Travel Sacred. Cousineau, Phil

Work Out: Calling people of faith into meaningful relationships. Hahn, Peggy, Krueger, Kristen and White, Rozella

Evangelical Lutheran Worship, 2006

Additional Resources

Books:

Change Your Questions, Change Your Life: 10 Powerful Tools for Life and Work. Adams, Marilee

The 4 Disciplines of Execution: Achieving Your Wildly Important Goals. McChesney, Chris, Covey, Sean, and Huling, Jim

Wake Up: Calling people of faith into God's Mission. Hahn, Peggy

The Sacred Valley: A guide for growing leaders with a deep, bold, consequential faith in Jesus Christ. Hahn, Peggy

The Practice of Adaptive Leadership: Tools and Tactics for Changing Your Organization and the World. Heifetz, Ronald, Grashow, Alexander and Linsky, Marty

Online resources:

Creativity and constraint by Yahoo CEO Marissa Meyers. YouTube video: Top 10 Rules for Success: https://www.youtube.com/watch?v=02zYZ-JB2zQ.

ELCA Ministry of Accompaniment. http://download.elca.org/ELCA%20Resource%20Repository/ACCOMPANIMENT_BIBLE_STUDY_INTRODUCTION_PAGES.pdf?

SMART Goals. https://www.mindtools.com/pages/article/smart-goals.htm

Listen in the Silence by singer/songwriter Linnea Good. http://www.linneagood.com/

Awakenings Movement. http://www.awakeningsmovement.com/

Go to waytolead.org/metrics for resources referred to in this field guide.

Enter access code:

PX36b3pQJY

Dedication

This book is dedicated to the leaders who will dare to use adaptive practices to unlock the creativity in the church for a deeper, more vibrant expression of God's love in the world.

Gratitude

Deep, bold, consequential faith is a gift that is passed from person to person. LEAD is deeply grateful for people who are willing to try. We give a heartfelt thanks to God for our parents, grandparents, and to those who stand in the place of parents, who raised us to take risks, ask questions, and lead.

Edward and Phyllis Dusang
Edward and Myrtle Dusang
John and Rita Mayer
Kenneth and Martha Tjornehoj
Arlynn and Nancy Hartfiel
Margaret Blade

We honor these people who have invested in our lives, along with all the others, because we believe that parenting, mentoring, and living out our faith in community is essential to being God's people.

Biography

Peggy Hahn is a passionate champion for growing leaders. She dreams of confident, Spirit-led leaders of all ages and cultures using their gifts to be the church in their own neighborhoods.

Peggy has served as the assistant to the Bishop in the Texas-Louisiana Gulf Coast Synod of the ELCA for 18 years. Prior to that, she served in three congregations in two states as an innovative lay leader and Deacon.

Peggy is the executive director of LEAD, since it was envisioned in 2012. This nonprofit organization is focused on resourcing and coaching church leaders who want to make adaptive changes.

Peggy received the 2014 Tom Hunstad award and has served the ELCA Youth Ministry Network as a coach to the board, a frequent workshop leader and intensive care course teacher. She has written six books, coordinated service projects for 36,000 and 32,000 people at the 2009 & 2012 ELCA Youth Gatherings in New Orleans. She was the innovator of Camp Hope Day Camp Ministries and The Disciple Project.

Peggy has made her enthusiasm for the gospel known in the U.S. and around the globe. She has led groups to Spanish-speaking countries for more than 24 years and is learning the language. She has survived being hit by a motorcycle in Africa, has hiked the Inca Trail in Peru, and has eaten papoosas with dear friends in El Salvador for 28 years. She walked the Camino de Santiago in 2016 and looks forward to more adventures in the future.

Peggy is married to Dewayne Hahn, lives in Houston, hangs out in the country in Smithville on weekends off, and calls New Orleans home. She loves gardening, reading, yoga, walking, and any time she gets to spend with their five adult children, their spouses, and six grandchildren.

Online resources at waytolead.org/metrics

Chapter	Page	Topic
Intro	19	Stories of revitalizing congregations
Intro	21	Sample designs for using this field guide in retreat or over several months
1	29	Samples of dashboards
1	34	Spiritual practices
2	40	Metrics to consider and designing digital dashboards
2	41	24-hour metrics retreat with question thinking
3	44	Order Value Cards
3	44	Outline for values workshop
4	64	Sample goals and metrics (related to congregational practices)
4	64	Setting goals and metrics for worship
4	64	Setting goals and metrics as we partner (with neighbor)
4	65	Setting goals and metrics for spirituality
4	65	Setting goals and metrics for community
4	65	Setting goals and metrics as we care (for each other)
4	66	Setting goals and metrics for generosity
4	66	Setting goals and metrics for leadership
4	70	SOAR process
5	76	Congregational stories of opening the doors
5	76	Building as a goal
5	77	Deep hospitality
6	85	Tips on brainstorming
6	90	Spiritual Types
6	90	Deepening Adult Faith
6	92-93	Print-ready metrics worksheets
7	101	Impact the bottom line
9	120	Vertical and horizontal intersection Worksheets

40486341R00077

Made in the USA
Middletown, DE
27 March 2019